Roman Emperors

A Guide to the Men Who Ruled the Empire

Mario Bartolini

PEN & SWORD
HISTORY

First published in Great Britain in 2023 by
Pen & Sword Military
An imprint of Pen & Sword Books Limited
Yorkshire – Philadelphia

Copyright © Mario Bartolini 2023

ISBN 978 1 39906 366 1

Typeset by Mac Style
Printed in the UK by CPI Group (UK) Ltd, Croydon, CR0 4YY.

MIX
Paper | Supporting
responsible forestry
FSC
www.fsc.org   FSC® C013604

Pen & Sword Books Limited incorporates the imprints of After the
Battle, Atlas, Archaeology, Aviation, Discovery, Family History,
Fiction, History, Maritime, Military, Military Classics, Politics,
Select, Transport, True Crime, Air World, Frontline Publishing,
Leo Cooper, Remember When, Seaforth Publishing, The Praetorian
Press, Wharncliffe Local History, Wharncliffe Transport,
Wharncliffe True Crime and White Owl.

For a complete list of Pen & Sword titles please contact

PEN & SWORD BOOKS LIMITED
47 Church Street, Barnsley, South Yorkshire, S70 2AS, England
E-mail: enquiries@pen-and-sword.co.uk
Website: www.pen-and-sword.co.uk
or
PEN AND SWORD BOOKS
1950 Lawrence Rd, Havertown, PA 19083, USA
E-mail: Uspen-and-sword@casematepublishers.com
Website: www.penandswordbooks.com

Contents

Introduction

The history of the classical Roman State spanned more than twelve centuries. It extended from the foundation of Rome in 753 BCE to the fall of the western part of the Empire in 476 CE. The rich legacy left by the Romans represents for the Western World much more than a distant historical reference. We only have to reflect on the origin of the systems of law, the Latin-based languages, the religious beliefs, as well as the collective social philosophy that are found there. It was also under the footsteps of the mighty legions that the foundations of modern European nations were forged. Several modern European capital cities were either intentionally founded in premeditated locations or were originally strategically located Roman military camps or outposts. The classical Roman State, whose cultural essence had its roots in ancient Greece, can undoubtedly be seen as the origin of Western civilization.

Like any great civilization, the Roman State experienced its share of diversity and fluctuations in its social order. Periods of violence and cruelty that sometimes went beyond modern comprehension were combined with times when peace, prosperity and refinement radiated the civilizing benefits of the Roman model.

The Roman political system also evolved during its existence. The first political framework instituted was a monarchy. From 753 to 509 BCE the Latin kings, Sabines and Etruscans made Rome grow and garnished it with its first monuments. From 509 to 27 BCE, this time as a republic, the Roman State provided itself with solid social and political infrastructures. The Roman Republic initiated a dynamic military and cultural expansion to soon occupy most of Europe, North Africa and the Middle East. After a period of internal struggles which eventually dismantled the foundations of the Republic, the Roman Empire was established in 27 BCE and ruled the Western-known world until 476 CE.

This book is a chronological guide of the individuals who ruled the Empire from 27 BCE until its fall in the West in 476 CE. Relevant information in the form of narratives is also added to help situate certain important individuals, historical events and to provide context. The words in italics in the text refer to a term or an emperor cited elsewhere in the book. The dates are all CE unless otherwise indicated.

One notion deserves to be mentioned here. In the collective consciousness of the Ancient Romans, the memory of the achievements of the dictator Julius Caesar (100–44 BCE) and of the first Roman emperor Augustus (63 BCE-14 CE) were such that the names of the two men became synonymous with distinction and status after their death. Three centuries later, when Emperor Diocletian (285–305) established the Tetrarchy, the Empire was then led by four co-emperors. In order to distinguish the hierarchy that existed between them, the two predominant emperors took the official title of Augustus and the other two, who were in fact deputies, were designated as Caesars. This explains the frequency of the use of these terms in this book, especially during the early Dominate period (285–395 CE).

Chronological Table

The Principate (27 BCE-285 CE)

	Birth and Death	Reign
Augustus	63 BCE-14 CE	27–14
Tiberius	42 BCE-37 CE	14–37
Caligula	12–41	37–41
Claudius	10 BCE-54 CE	41–54
Nero	37–68	54–68
Galba	3 BCE-69 CE	68–69
Otho	32–69	69
Vitellius	15–69	69
Vespasian	9–79	69–79
Titus	39–81	79–81
Domitian	51–96	81–96
Nerva	30–98	96–98
Trajan	53–117	98–117
Hadrian	76–138	117–138
Antoninus Pius	86–161	138–161
Marcus Aurelius	121–180	161–180
Lucius Verus	130–169	161–169
Commodus	161–192	180–192
Pertinax	126–193	193
Didius Julianus	133–193	193
Septimius Severus	146–211	193–211
Geta	189–211	211
Caracalla	188–217	211–217
Macrinus	164–218	217–218
Elagabalus	204–222	218–222

Severus Alexander	208–235	222–235
Maximinus Thrax	173–238	235–238
Gordian I	157–238	238
Gordian II	192–238	238
Pupienus	164–238	238
Balbinus	178–238	238
Gordian III	225–244	238–244
Philip the Arab	204–249	244–249
Decius	201–251	249–251
Trebonianus Gallus	206–253	251–253
Aemilian	207–253	253
Valerian	195–260	253–260
Gallienus	218–268	253–268
Claudius Gothicus	214–270	268–270
Aurelian	214–275	270–275
Tacitus	200–276	275–276
Florian	?-276	276
Probus	232–282	276–282
Carus	222–283	282–283
Numerian	253–284	283–284
Carinus	250–285	283–285

The Early Dominate (285–395)

Diocletian	244–311	284–305
Maximian	250–310	286–305 and 306–310
Constantius Chlorus	250–306	305–306
Galerius	260–311	305–311
Valerius Severus	?-307	306–307
Maxentius	283–312	306–312
Licinius	265–324	307–324
Maximinus Daia	270–313	310–313
Constantine I	272–337	306–337
Constantine II	316–340	337–340
Constans I	323–350	337–350
Constantius II	317–361	337–361

Magnentius	303–353	350–353
Julian	331–363	361–363
Jovian	331–364	363–364
Valentinian I	321–375	364–375
Valens	328–378	364–378
Gratian	359–383	367–383
Valentinian II	371–392	375–392
Magnus Maximus	335–388	383–388
Theodosius I	347–395	379–395

Western Emperors (395–476)

Honorius	384–423	395–423
Constantius III	?-421	421
Johannes	?-425	423–425
Valentinian III	419–455	425–455
Petronius Maximus	396–455	455
Avitus	385–457	455–456
Majorian	420–461	457–461
Libius Severus	?-465	461–465
Anthemius	420–472	467–472
Olybrius	420–472	472
Glycerius	?-?	473–474
Julius Nepos	430–480	474–475
Romulus Augustus	460–?	475–476

Eastern Emperors (395–491)

Arcadius	377–408	395–408
Theodosius II	401–450	408–450
Marcian	396–457	450–457
Leo I	401–474	457–474
Zeno	425–491	474–491

Rome Before the Empire
and Dynastic Narratives

Aeneas

Archaeological discoveries of the last decades demonstrate that the first colonization of the Lazio region of Italy dates back to the twelfth century BCE. According to legend, Aeneas, son of Aphrodite, escaped the destruction of Troy and left Ionia with his companions. After a long and perilous voyage at sea, they arrived at the banks of the river Tiber. Once on the future site of Rome, Aeneas joined a local chief named Evander. The latter, originally from Arcadia, had already founded a Greek town, Pallanteum, on a hill which would later bear the name of Palatine. Aeneas and his companions settled on a nearby hill and founded Lavinium. Stimulated by trade, these villages made up of shepherds and fishermen developed rapidly. Over time, these towns amalgamated, giving birth to a nation that would be called upon to dominate the Western world.

Monarchy

(753–509 BCE)

Tradition has it that Romulus, considered the first king of Rome, founded the city in 753 BCE. Gradually, the surrounding hills and valleys became covered with dwellings and public buildings. Because of their proximity, the Etruscan confederation in the north and the Greek colonies in the south of the Italian peninsula greatly influenced Rome culturally.

According to legend, Romulus conducted the initial organization of the city. It was based on a senatorial body which assisted and advised the warrior chief. It was Romulus who initiated the war against a neighbouring people of the Latins, the Sabines. This conflict concluded with the victory of the Latins, and a merging of the two peoples ensued. To succeed Romulus, the Senate chose a Sabine named Numa Pompilius. The latter gave Rome a public law system and the basis of the Roman religion strongly influenced by the Greek religion. His successor, Tullus Hostilius, established the law of war. It was within the context of this ritual that the battle took place between the three Horatii, champions of Rome, and the Curiatii, champions of Alba. The defeat of Alba triggered a further enlargement of the dominion of Rome. Tullus Hostilius's successor was Numa's grandson, Ancus Martius. He rose to the throne in 639 BCE. He built the first wooden bridge over the Tiber and established settlers in Ostia, a port located at the mouth of the Tiber River which flows into the Tyrrhenian Sea. When he died in 616 BCE, another era in Roman history began.

At the end of the seventh century BCE, Etruscan influence became more important in the region. In fact, two of the last three kings of Rome were Etruscan and they transformed the city into an urban centre. Lucius Tarquinius, or Tarquinius the Elder, was elected king after the death of Ancus Martius. His reign, which ended in 579 BCE, was marked by significant construction work. He established a sewage system, thus giving the Romans their first contact with urban sanitation. This concept of urban cleanliness and, subsequently, that of personal hygiene was to become an integral part of what was to define being a Roman citizen. Lucius Tarquinius also undertook the construction of the temple of Jupiter on the Capitol Hill.

Murdered by the descendants of Ancus, Lucius Tarquinius was replaced by a Latin, Servius Tullius. King from 578 to 535 BCE, Servius established social classes within Roman society and forged the census system. Military service adapted according to the ranks of the citizens, and Servius surrounded the Seven Hills of Rome with continuous ramparts. In 535 BCE, Servius was assassinated by the sons of Tarquinius the Elder. One of them, Lucius Tarquinius Superbus, or Tarquinius the Superb, seized power and reigned until 509 BCE. He completed the construction of the temple of Jupiter. A good war chief, he was also the typical model of a tyrant whose authority was based on force. His pride and excesses made him a hated figure of authority. In 509 BCE, he was driven out of Rome and a Republic was established. This new regime was to persist for five centuries.

Republic

(509–27 BCE)

The citizens of Rome ousted their last king in 509 BCE, power was divided between the magistrates, the Senate and the assemblies of the people. This partition of authority, which characterized the institutional system of the Republic, was intended to create a balance of power and prevent the return of any autocratic type of authority. Following the erosion of the Etruscan hegemony around 474 BCE, Rome broke away from its yoke of authority. Following a game of alliances and a period of wars which lasted two centuries (including the Samnite wars from 343 to 290 BCE), Rome imposed its domination on the italic tribes of central Italy and even on its former masters, the Etruscans. Subsequently, the Roman conquest of the Greek colonies in the south of the peninsula was completed with the fall of Taranto in 271 BCE. Rome, mistress of most of the peninsula, soon came up against its biggest rival to date: Carthage. It was after the harsh Punic Wars (264–146 BCE) that Rome submitted its last great adversary in the West. Having become a formidable military power, Rome set out to conquer the entire Mediterranean world. Eventually, Greece, Asia Minor, Judea, Spain and Gaul became Roman provinces.

For four centuries, the republican regime worked well, but internal struggles, partly due to the increase of social inequities between the wealthy and the poor, started to gradually ruin its structures, thus favouring the return to autocracy. Marius (107–86 BCE) then Sylla (82–79 BCE), who were the first representatives of this return to a centralization of power, headed the State with the support of the army. Around 70 BCE, a series of external troubles, such as the servile revolt of Spartacus and the revolts in Pontus and in Judea, triggered new military expeditions. Once peace was restored, the generals glorified by military victories competed for dominance of public and political life in Rome. This was the case of Crassus, Pompey and *Caesar*. In

60 BCE, the three powerful men allied and formed a triumvirate. When Crassus was killed in 53 BCE during a military campaign against the Parthians, the fragile balance was broken. A civil war broke out between the partisans of Pompey and those of *Caesar*. In 48 BCE, Pompey was defeated, and *Caesar* became dictator, sole head of the Roman State. After his assassination in 44 BCE, the civil wars resumed for his succession. In 43 BCE, Mark Anthony, Lepidus and *Octavian* formed a second triumvirate and marched on Rome. Their victory over the republican legions representing the Senate was decisive: the Republic was agonizing. The rivalry soon appeared between the three men. Once Lepidus was removed from power when the triumvirate expired in 33 BCE, conflict erupted between Mark Anthony and *Octavian*. In 31 BCE, at the Battle of Actium, Mark Anthony with Cleopatra as an ally, was beaten. *Octavian* returned to Rome triumphant and, in 27 BCE, the Senate gave him the title of *Augustus*. It was the beginning of the Empire which was to last until 476 CE.

Marius *Caius Marius*

Arpinum (Arpino), Italy 157 BCE – Rome, Italy 86 BCE

Roman general heir to the philosophy of the Gracchi brothers, Marius was favourable to the cause of the plebs. This champion of the people gathered around him the dissatisfied and the under-represented of society. After a career as a magistrate, he became consul in 107 BCE. Marius carried out a major reform of the army by admitting the previously excluded poor. The poor gradually replaced the peasants and the wealthy owners in the legion, thus making it a professional army. This army, which was now entirely devoted to its leader, changed the balance of power between the Senate and the army. Indeed, this new political reality, where senatorial authority was reduced, was a prelude to the gradual process of the advent of the Empire. The military successes of Marius against the Berbers and Germanic tribes led the Senate to appoint him proconsul in 105 BCE. The aristocracy, injured by the reforms of Marius in favour of the plebs, had its own representative in the person of *Sulla*. This very ambitious character took advantage of a turnaround favourable to the aristocracy to supersede Marius and take his place as the dominant figure on the political scene.

Sulla *Lucius Cornelius*

Cumae (Cumes), Italy 138 BCE – Cumae (Cumes), Italy 78 BCE

Delegate then rival of *Marius*, Sulla took advantage of external troubles such as the revolt of Mithridates VI, King of Pont, and of the internal disorder due to the plebeian reforms of the Gracchi and *Marius* to be designated dictator by the aristocracy. In 82 BCE, after crushing his opponents, he was assigned a dictatorship for life. At the height of his prestige and his authority, he suddenly withdrew from political life in 79 BCE, to die the following year. The concentration of power in personal authority performed by *Marius* and Sulla at the expense of the Senate demonstrated the decline of the republican system. The authority of the generals began to take precedence over the Roman political chessboard. This concentration of power was the prelude of the imminent fall of the Republic, the first step toward the establishment of the Empire.

Caesar *Caius Julius Caesar*

Rome, Italy 100 BCE – Rome, Italy 44 BCE

Nephew of *Marius*, Caesar was a patrician linked to the plebeian cause. He embarked on a political career by exploiting both the upper class and popular discontent. His fame on the political scene was completed by military successes in Spain. Having become very influential, he was part in 60 BCE of a triumvirate with two other powerful men, Crassus and Pompey. Once elected consul, he undertook the conquest of Gaul (58–51 BCE) thus gaining military glory and a loyal army. When Crassus died in 53 BCE, ambition began to dictate the conduct of the remaining two generals and war soon became inevitable. In 49 BCE, Caesar defied a senatorial ban and marched on Rome with his army in order to take power, thus causing a civil war against the troops of the Senate and of Pompey. Victorious,

Caesar was proclaimed consul and dictator for life. No doubt tempted by the diadem of the monarch, Caesar was assassinated by senators in 44 BCE. His exploits and his mark in the collective mind were such that his name later became synonymous with greatness. The events surrounding the dictatorships of *Marius* and *Sulla* were trying experiences for the republican system where control of political authority began to slip out of the Senate's hands. The civil war and the following dictatorship of Caesar highlighted the inability of the Senate to restore order and preserve its authority, which was fading before the growing power of the generals. The context was therefore favourable for the establishment of an autocratic regime.

Julio-Claudians

From Augustus (27 BCE) to Nero (68 CE)

Originating from *Caesar*, it was the first imperial dynasty of ancient Rome. Its members were the emperors *Augustus*, *Tiberius*, *Caligula*, *Claudius* and *Nero*. With these emperors, the Empire took a legitimate form, and we witnessed the beginning of the formation of a centralized administrative and financial system. This robust imperial apparatus was responsible for the establishment and preservation of social balance and, among other things, the stable balance between State revenues and expenditures, which was to persist for two centuries. The Julio-Claudians provided Rome and the whole of Italy with remarkable construction. In addition, trade was flourishing, and gold was circulating well. The Roman model was exported to the provinces, where it quickly took root. It was the beginning of Roman 'universalism' in Europe.

The borders of the Roman world were widened, and we witnessed the beginning of their progressive integration with the erection of the *limes*, which were the fortified borders of the Empire with no natural defences. Supreme authority rested on the exercise of military command, but the support of the Senate and the active presence of the aristocracy on the political scene confirmed a consolidation of power. Succession was ensured by the adoption of a candidate by the emperor, which was followed by the formal sanction of the Senate.

Flavians

From Vespasian (69) to Domitian (96)

This very short but significant dynasty of Roman emperors included *Vespasian*, *Titus* and *Domitian*. Subsequent to the troubles following *Nero*'s death, *Vespasian* founded this brief hereditary dynasty by becoming emperor after being acclaimed by the army. Originating from the Italian 'bourgeoisie', the Flavians succeeded in putting an end to the civil war and in restoring order to the finances of the State. They thus maintained the socio-economic balance of the Empire instituted by the *Julio-Claudians*. Reforms were made to the tax collection system and construction work spread to the provinces, where new roads were built. The predominance of the Italian aristocracy on the political scene began to decline with the arrival of 'Romanized' provincials in Rome, thus further homogenizing the elites.

Antonines

From Nerva (96) to Commodus (192)

The members of the Antonine imperial dynasty were *Nerva*, *Trajan*, *Hadrian*, *Antoninus Pius*, *Marcus Aurelius*, *Lucius Verus* and *Commodus*. When *Trajan* became emperor in 98, he was the first emperor of non-Italian origin. The reigns of the Antonines represented the golden age of the Empire. At the heart of the *Pax romana*, the social and financial equilibrium of the State was at full maturity. The cultural influence of the Roman world was perceived as far as India. It was under *Trajan* that the last great Roman military conquests took place. With the annexation of Dacia (modern Romania), Armenia and Mesopotamia, the Empire reached the greatest geographic extent in its history. By the same token, the 'natural' physical limits of the Empire were reached, since any additional territorial expansion would have made the Empire difficult to govern and almost impossible to defend with the 'technical' means and resources of the time. The priority of the Antonines then turned to strengthening the defensive structure of the Empire. The reign of *Commodus* concluded an era in the history of the Empire. The social and financial balance maintained for more than a century began to show signs of strain. The considerable weakening of the aristocracy and of the authority of the Senate prompted the degradation of the Principate system inaugurated by *Augustus* and signalled the prelude to a military monarchy that eventually erased all pretence of civil authority from the Empire.

Severans

From Septimius Severus (193) to Severus Alexander (235)

The Severans represented a dynasty of Roman emperors, which was temporarily interrupted by the short reign of *Macrinus*, whose members were *Septimius Severus*, *Geta*, *Caracalla*, *Elagabalus* and *Severus Alexander*. During this period, the economic situation of the Empire was generally good. This period witnessed the appearance of new taxes and the disappearance of important exemptions reserved for the aristocracy. However, the currency began to lose its value and its circulation decreased. The scarcity of precious metals and the decline in trade, caused by the impoverishment of the aristocracy, were undoubtedly among the causes. Since the time of the *Antonines*, different sects had evolved within the Empire and some had merged with the Roman religion. This natural evolution to religious syncretism was a step toward monotheism, an important cultural aspect which would later characterize the fourth century and prepare mentalities for the advent of Christianity. The social homogeneity of the various peoples of the Empire was at its peak, and Italy's pre-eminence in stature over the rest of the provinces, if it still existed, was no longer visible.

Three distinctive features defined this dynasty. First, as a general rule, the Severans governed as absolute monarchs, thus excluding the Senate from the decision-making process. The civil facade of the authority represented by the reign of an emperor who collaborated with the Senate, a normality under the *Julio-Claudians*, *Flavians* and *Antonines*, evaporated. The process of centralizing power was complete, and the State intervened in almost all spheres of society. Second, the Severans devoted significant resources to the army. They granted numerous privileges and substantial increases in pay, so that the general condition of the military improved considerably. The influence of the military was greatly increased at the expense of what was left of senatorial authority. The army now represented the main lever of the emperor's authority on the political spectrum. Finally, in connection with the obliteration of the Senate, the aristocracy hard hit by the Severans was also impoverished and even, according to some historians, reduced in numbers. This situation had major repercussions at the death of *Severus Alexander*. In 235, a political vacuum was created, and a serious crisis ensued. The weak positions of the aristocracy and the Senate in the political arena left the way open for the military to compete for power. This crisis, dubbed 'military anarchy' by historians, was to last fifty years and shook the Empire to its foundations. On the other side of the *limes*, the growing population of the Germanic tribes, which in contact with the Romans had begun to organize and settle down, created an ever-increasing pressure on the Empire's defence apparatus. This permanent threat of invasion already visible under *Marcus Aurelius* became one of the major concerns of the Severan emperors. From that point on, this new reality inevitably affected the history of the Empire until its fall in the West.

Emperors of the Principate (27 BCE-285 CE)

Augustus *Caius Julius Caesar Octavius*

Rome, Italy 63 BCE – Nola, Italy 14 CE
Reign: 27 BCE-14 CE

O riginating from a family of the equestrian order, Octavian was admitted to high nobility by alliance. Wishing to make his nephew Octavian a future politician, Julius *Caesar* worked diligently in favour of his career development and provided him with an excellent education. In 45 BCE, *Caesar* adopted him. When *Caesar* was assassinated the following year, the young Octavian, then 19 years old, began his ascent to the supreme authority. Following intrigue and armed clashes, Octavian was elected consul and with Lepidus and Mark Anthony formed a triumvirate in 43 BCE. When this arrangement expired in 33 BCE, Lepidus was removed from the political scene. The struggle then became inevitable between the ambitious Octavian, master of the western part of the Roman

Silver Denarius of Augustus.

world, and Mark Anthony who, with the support of Cleopatra, the Queen of independent Egypt, governed the East. Octavian's victory at Actium in 31 BCE, followed by the progressive conquest of the East, pushed Mark Anthony and Cleopatra to suicide. Egypt then became a Roman province. Following these events, Octavian entered Rome as the sole master of the Roman world.

Not wanting the return of a *monarchy*, a concept linked to the memory of the Tarquinii kings that the Romans particularly despised, and remembering the fate experienced by *Caesar*, Octavian aspired to be 'summoned' by the Senate to legitimize his authority. Public opinion and the socio-political context were ripe. Tired of the civil wars which had shaken society for the past dozen years, the Romans wanted the return of stability. In 27 BCE, the Senate granted Octavian the title of Augustus, which became an integral part of his name. The powers hitherto held by the various magistrates were now conferred upon him. The Empire was established, and Augustus, on a basis of authority which was still fragile, initiated the *Julio-Claudian* dynasty.

The first Roman emperor tried to reintegrate ancient values and traditions into Roman society. He restored some prestige to the Senate despite the fact that in reality its political authority remained limited. The Empire was administered by a corps of officials coming from the upper classes of society. Augustus reorganized the Empire by forming senatorial and imperial provinces, the latter being under the direct authority of the emperor. The civil servant hierarchy quickly adapted to the new context, which facilitated the management of Roman lands. The army was also reorganized: The number of legions was set at 25, and military service increased from sixteen to twenty years. The upper ranks were filled by senators and knights, but soldiers of the lower classes had the opportunity to climb to the respectable rank of centurion. In order to support the consolidation of his authority, Augustus established the Praetorian Guard, an elite armed body charged with protecting the emperor.

Augustus completed the pacification of Spain and pushed the border of the Empire to the Danube River. The relatively moderate foreign policy of Augustus became prudent following the treachery of Teutoburg in year 9. It is during this large-scale ambush that Varus perished, faithful lieutenant of the emperor, and three legions in the hands of a coalition of Germanic tribes. This military catastrophe forever marked the collective Roman spirit and crystallized apprehensions toward the Germanic tribes for the rest of Antiquity.

Eager to leave the Empire in the hands of a competent man after his death, Augustus experimented with different people and formulas. His first hopes rested on an old friend, Agrippa, who married Julia, the emperor's own daughter. But Agrippa died in 12 BCE. Augustus then turned his attention to his two grandsons, Caius and Lucius *Caesar*, but they died in years 2 and 4 respectively. It is then that Augustus adopted *Tiberius*, son of his wife Livia from a previous marriage. By year 13, *Tiberius* held almost all of the levers of power, given the advanced age of Augustus. *Tiberius* succeeded him a year later, when Augustus died at the age of 77.

The accomplishments of Augustus were remarkable. The Empire acquired a legitimate form and was very well organized. Even if the authority of the Empire ultimately rested on the absolute exercise of military command, which could be a weakness in difficult circumstances, the presence of the Senate nevertheless ensured a certain balance in the division of powers. Thanks to the achievements of Augustus, his principate corresponded to one of the most brilliant periods in Roman history, hence the hailed expression 'Century of Augustus'.

Tiberius *Tiberius Julius Caesar*

Rome, Italy 42 BCE – Misenum (Miseno), Italy 37
Reign: 14–37
Tiberius was the son of Livia who married *Augustus* in a second marriage. In search of a successor, *Augustus* adopted Tiberius in year 4. Very quickly, Tiberius demonstrated his qualities by fighting in Germania and Illyria. When Agrippa died in year 12, Tiberius was persuaded by the emperor to marry the widow, Julia, the daughter of *Augustus*. Tiberius was associated with the Empire the following year. Becoming emperor upon the death of *Augustus*, Tiberius governed by

Silver Denarius of Tiberius.

sharing the power with the Senate. According to the wishes of the late emperor, Tiberius adopted Germanicus, *Augustus*'s nephew, with the aim of making him his eventual successor despite the fact that he himself already had a son named Drusus. Tiberius was competent, conscientious and exercised rigorous financial administration. However, in the face of revolts within the army, he gradually adopted an authoritarian and suspicious behaviour.

In year 16, Germanicus carried out a punitive expedition in Germania against Arminius, thus avenging the treachery of Teutoburg. He therefore pushed back the frontiers of the Empire on the Rhine and brought back to Rome the standards of the three legions annihilated seven years earlier. He also created two new provinces in the East (Cappadocia and Commagene), while Drusus carried out expeditions against the king of Bohemia. Shortly after these victories, Germanicus died suddenly in Egypt.

In 27, having become ill, Tiberius withdrew to the island of Capri, leaving the management of State affairs to the Praetorian prefect Sejanus, who quickly began to covet power. Sejanus even poisoned Drusus, the son of Tiberius, in order to prepare his usurpation. Realizing Sejanus's ambitious aims, Tiberius retook the reins of power and had him executed in 31. Because of Tiberius's behaviour, who was embittered by these events, the last six years of his principate were presented by certain historians as a difficult period. His constant, even sickly concern to avoid conspiracies and to keep control of the finances of the Empire pushed him to accuse numerous dignitaries, including his relatives, whom he considered too greedy or ambitious.

As a general rule, Tiberius's policy aligned with those of *Augustus* despite a sometimes tumultuous relationship with the Senate. A stern and suspicious man to his entourage, Tiberius remained a very competent man at the head of the Empire to which he continued to show sincere integrity until his death in 37. At the age of 78, Tiberius died of natural causes despite rumours of murder.

Caligula *Caius Caesar Augustus Germanicus*

Antium (Anzio), Italy 12 – Rome, Italy 41
Reign: 37–41

Son of Germanicus adopted by *Tiberius*, Caius was a young man with fragile physical and mental health and who was unknown until then. When still a child, Caius accompanied Germanicus on military expeditions. Often dressed as a little soldier, Caius also wore small military sandals called caligae. Lovingly, the soldiers who saw him parading on horseback with his father nicknamed him Caligula, meaning 'little sandals'. He succeeded *Tiberius* on his death in 37.

Sestertius of Caligula.

The young 25-year-old emperor had neither the personal ability nor the skills to govern. Rather obsessed with carnal pleasures and oriental esotericism, he remained very far from the reality of power and the needs of the Empire. His unpredictable temper and thirst for sadism and extravagance quickly became legendary. Leading the fashion of the oriental despot surrounded by mysticism, the unbalanced young man undertook many urban projects, only to abandon them almost immediately. Governing according to his fortuitous emotions, in 39 he ordered an expedition to Germania without a precise military motive and without significant strategic consequences. The arbitrary assassinations of foreign governors and dignitaries pushed certain provinces such as Mauritania, Armenia and Judea toward instability, even open revolt.

In 40, the Senate, openly despised by Caligula, and various levels of Roman authority considered getting rid of the emperor. However, the latter retained the most important support: that of the army. Less affected by his depraved actions, the legions remained loyal to him. However, once the Praetorian Guard was pushed into the ranks of the opponents, a conspiracy fomented by senators, members of the equestrian order and Praetorian officers put an end to the insane reign of Caligula, despite the support of the majority of the army. Caligula was assassinated at the age of 29. The solid foundations of the imperial regime established by *Augustus* and consolidated by *Tiberius* resisted this first interlude of inconsistency and insanity.

Claudius *Tiberius Caesar Augustus Germanicus*

Lugdunum (Lyon), France 10 BCE – Rome, Italy 54 CE
Reign: 41–54
Emperor *Caligula*'s assassination in 41 generated a controversy. The Senate wished to restore the Republic, while the Praetorians wanted to maintain the status quo. Eventually, Germanicus's brother Claudius was designated to succeed his nephew. Present in the imperial entourage since *Augustus*, he had been kept in the background of political life because of physical handicaps. Having a rather obvious gait due to a malformation of a leg and afflicted with stuttering,

Silver Tetradrachm of Claudius.

Claudius was nevertheless a highly cultivated man and carried out an impressive number of literary works during his life.

Once Claudius became emperor, his moderation and his concern for the well-being of the Empire made him an administrator and a leader comparable to *Augustus* despite his changing personality. He developed the central administration and worked to expand and consolidate the Empire. Claudius encouraged the establishment of Roman colonies in the old cities of the Empire and the foundation of new cities according to the Roman model. This practice had been initiated by *Augustus* and had continued thereafter. The construction of aqueducts, new roads and the extension of old ones boosted the economy and helped the political and administrative cohesion of the Empire. The right to Roman citizenship was extended in the pacified and stable provinces.

Statue of Claudius I in Delphi.

Claudius had to invest a lot of energy and resources to repair the bungles of his predecessor. He suppressed the revolts in Mauritania, Thrace and Judea and was much-admired for the conquest of Britannia (present-day England) and Lycia (South-West of Asia Minor) in 43. Germanic incursions into the *limes* of the Rhine were also repulsed.

Strongly cultivated but weak in character, he allowed himself to be dominated by his third wife, Messalina, then by his fourth, Agrippina, daughter of his brother Germanicus. After adopting her son *Nero*, he witnessed multiple intrigues starting to surface around him. Agrippina eventually poisoned Claudius and dismissed Britannicus, son of Claudius and Messalina, from power to place on the throne her own son, *Nero*. In reality, this ambitious woman aimed to grasp power by governing on behalf of young *Nero*.

Nero *Nero Claudius Drusus Germanicus Caesar*

Antium, (Anzio), Italy 37 – Rome, Italy 68
Reign: 54–68

Son of Agrippina, Nero was adopted by *Claudius*, whom he succeeded at the age of 17 even if at the beginning, his mother Agrippina reigned in his place. Despite the assassination of Britannicus, son and legitimate successor of *Claudius*, in 55, and later that of his own distressing mother Agrippina, in 59, the early stages of the Principate

Gold Aureus of Nero.

of this cultivated young man surrounded by good advisors remained favourable.

After the death of Burrus, Praetorian prefect, advisor and friend of Nero, followed by the disgrace of Seneca, a tax collector compromised in a conspiracy against Nero, in 62, the young emperor succumbed to an unregulated despotism. That same year, driven by his own emotions, he repudiated his wife Octavia, daughter of *Claudius*, whom he pushed to suicide with the aim of marrying Poppea, his mistress and wife of the general and future emperor *Otho*. In 65, he killed Poppea, then pregnant, in a fit of anger.

Nero arbitrarily condemned the wealthy to death in order to appropriate their property, thereby attempting to feed the State coffers emptied by imperial extravagances. He unleashed the first persecutions against the Christians, now dogmatically dissociated from the Jews in public opinion. He accused them of being responsible for the fire of Rome which, in 64, destroyed three quarters of the city. The external events that marked Nero's reign were the revolts in Armenia (54), Britannica and Judea (61), which were the consequences of his irrational political decisions. His unrealistic military aims in Ethiopia and the Caucasus were two other examples of such decisions.

This regime of terror gave rise to many conspiracies such as that of Piso in 65, which were in turn aborted. However, in 68, part of the army, under General *Galba* in Spain and General Vindex in Gaul, rose up against Nero. It was the first time that the army had betrayed its loyalty to the emperor. Declared a public enemy by the Senate, Nero killed himself, thus abruptly ending the *Julio-Claudian* dynasty and opening a period of civil war.

Galba *Servius Sulpicius*

Terracina, Italy, 3 BCE – Rome, Italy 69 CE
Reign: 68–69
In year 68, part of the army revolted against the depraved rule of Emperor *Nero*. Two generals led this revolt: Vindex and Galba. Vindex, of Gallo-Roman origin, was beaten and killed in a battle against the armies of the Rhine who wished to elect their own contender for the

Silver Denarius of Galba.

purple cloak. Following *Nero*'s suicide, Galba, with the help of his Spanish troops and the tacit agreement of the Praetorians, seized power with the consent of the Senate.

Even if Galba's family was not of imperial origin, he was greatly appreciated by *Augustus*, *Tiberius* and *Claudius*. He was proconsul of Africa under *Claudius* and then governor of Tarraconensis in modern-day Spain under *Nero*. Experienced in politics, the 70-year-old aristocrat nevertheless found it difficult to master the tumultuous social situation prevailing in Rome in 68. Poorly advised because of the incompetence of those who helped him become emperor and who now occupied important positions in the new administration, Galba committed a series of blunders which instigated his downfall. His first mistake was to consider his recent rise to power as a fait accompli. Imagining himself untouchable, Galba did not manoeuvre to consolidate his position. Furthermore, believing that he was carrying out a proper deed, the emperor had those responsible for the overthrow of *Nero* executed, possibly to discourage future undertakings of this kind. Unbeknownst to him, the conspiracy compromised many people, including very high dignitaries. Galba quickly made dangerous enemies. He also made the crucial mistake of refusing to pay the money owed to the Praetorians in exchange for their loyalty. This liberality was traditionally paid at the ascension of a new emperor. Galba lowered taxes and cut public spending considerably. This last financial measure, although logical under the circumstances, made the old emperor unpopular with the Roman people, who were used to the extravagant and disproportionate expenses of *Nero*.

Meanwhile, dissatisfied with the choice of emperor, the legions stationed in Germania, having defeated Vindex, in turn chose an emperor in the person of *Vitellius*. While negotiations were taking place between *Vitellius* and Emperor Galba, the latter was assassinated by the Praetorians from whom he had always refused to buy loyalty and who had just chosen their own emperor in the person of *Otho*. The Principate of Galba lasted seven months.

Otho *Marcus Salvius*

Ferentium (near Viterbo), Italy 32 – Brixellum (Brescello), Italy 69
Reign: 69
Discontented because *Galba* refused to pay the liberality traditionally attributed to them on the ascension of the new emperor, the Praetorians assassinated the old emperor and chose another: the young Otho, aged 37. Coming from a respectable family, Otho was in *Nero*'s entourage until 58. It was then that he had detached himself from the emperor's inner circle and was assigned to the post of governor of the distant province of Lusitania (modern Portugal). The end of

Silver Denarius of Otho.

this friendship was undoubtedly linked to the fact that Otho's wife Poppea had become *Nero*'s mistress.

Otho was quite capable of assuming his new role but had few opportunities to prove it because of the recent appointment of the commander of the Rhine legions, *Vitellius*, as emperor by his own troops. After attempts at conciliation to put an end to the civil war, Otho had to quickly react to an imminent invasion of Italy by the army of Germania. Otho, who had just legitimized his authority, had to organize the defence of Italy. The armies of the East and of Africa were loyal to Otho, but these legions were dispersed and far from the capital. The proximity of *Vitellius*'s legions made the situation critical. When the latter arrived in the north of the peninsula, the opposition presented to them by Otho boiled down to a single legion supported by Praetorian cohorts, a few detachments drafted in the vicinity and two thousand gladiators. After the fierce Battle of Bedriacum between the two unequal forces, Otho's army was defeated. Even though two of his legions were nearby and ready to intervene, Otho ordered his troops to stand down to stop the bloodshed. After a Principate of three months, in April 69, Otho carried out the 'heroic' gesture of committing suicide.

Vitellius *Aulus Vitellius Germanicus Augustus*

Luceria (Lucera), Italy 15 – Rome, Italy 69
Reign: 69

Without military experience, Vitellius had long been present in the imperial entourage. Consul and governor of Britannia under *Claudius*, he had been governor of Africa before taking civilian command of the Army of the Rhine under *Nero*. Son of a consul, Vitellius was proclaimed emperor by the legions stationed in Germania, which he commanded shortly after the death of *Nero*. At first, he hesitated to claim the purple cloak, but the death of *Galba* made him decide to march into Italy to fight *Otho*, to take the capital and legitimize his new title. Vitellius defeated *Otho* at the Battle of Bedriacum, but this victory was only partial because, despite *Otho*'s death, he did not have the support of the rest of the army. The civil war begun by the

Praetorian Guard that was fighting for its own survival continued. Even before *Vespasian* arrived in Rome, the city was invested; Vitellius was captured and killed.

Vespasian *Titus Flavius Vespasianus*

Falacrines (near Cittareale), Italy 9 – Aquae Cutiliae (near Cittaducale), Italy 79
Reign: 69–79
Military tribune in Thrace under *Tiberius*, Vespasian commanded a legion during the conquest of Britannia and assisted in pacifying it under *Claudius*. Under *Nero*, he began to quell the revolt in Judea which was not totally suppressed until 70 by his son *Titus*. On the death of *Nero*, Vespasian swore loyalty to *Galba*, then, following *Galba*'s death, to *Otho*. Faced with the apparent usurpation of *Vitellius*, commander of the Rhine legions, the army of the East proclaimed Vespasian emperor, in opposition. At the Battle of Cremona, *Vitellius*'s army was defeated by the army of the Danube, loyal to Vespasian. The latter was then confirmed in his new functions by the Senate even before his arrival in Rome. There is a major difference between Vespasian's takeover and that of his three predecessors: Vespasian succeeded in ending the civil war by ultimately obtaining unanimity in the army.

Silver Denarius of Vespasian.

Flavian Amphitheatre (Colosseum) in Rome.

Originating from the Italian middle-class, energetic and simple, the founder of the *Flavian* dynasty was genuine and realistic in the affairs of the State. Respectful toward the Senate from which he solicited advice, Vespasian was accessible, tolerant and apparently even expressed a good sense of humour. He built a reputation for tightfistedness by bringing order to the State's finances, which had been severely affected by *Nero*'s extravagant reign and the ensuing civil war. Tax collection was made more efficient with the help of a census in 73. The emperor reformed the central administration and reduced the influence of the Roman aristocracy by encouraging the entry of provincial nobles to the Senate. New construction was impressive. Vespasian rebuilt the Capitol, destroyed by the fires of 64 and 69, and began the construction of the *Flavian* amphitheatre, which would later take the name of Colosseum because of its colossal dimensions. He began paving the streets of Rome and stabilized the banks of the Tiber River which flows through it. Improving communications and transportation in the Empire was a major concern for the emperor. It was now common to see legionaries stationed at the edge of the Empire working on the construction of roads, bridges and the transformation of permanent wooden military camps into stone.

The emperor elevated his two sons *Titus* and *Domitian* to power, thus establishing a system of hereditary succession. In external affairs, activity was also intense. Revolts in Gaul, in Britannia and in Judea, consequences of the troubles of 68–69, were repressed. Vespasian widened Roman Britannia, pursued the pacification of Judea and undertook the conquest of the Agri Decumates (Decumatian Fields), a territory of strategic defence between the Rhine and the Upper Danube. The well-ordered and disciplined army resumed its former cohesion.

At the age of 69, Vespasian was in great physical and mental shape, but death struck unexpectedly. Suddenly feverish during a trip to Campania, in the south of Italy, he died as soon as he arrived at Aquae Cutiliae, where he had intended to take cold medicinal baths. For the first time since the death of *Augustus*, the memory of a dead emperor universally provoked grief and esteem throughout the Empire.

Titus *Titus Flavius Vespasianus*

Rome, Italy, 39 – Aquae Cutiliae (near Cittaducale), Italy 81
Reign: 79–81

Son of Emperor *Vespasian*, Titus was a military tribune in Germania and then in Britannia under *Nero*. He and his brother *Domitian* were

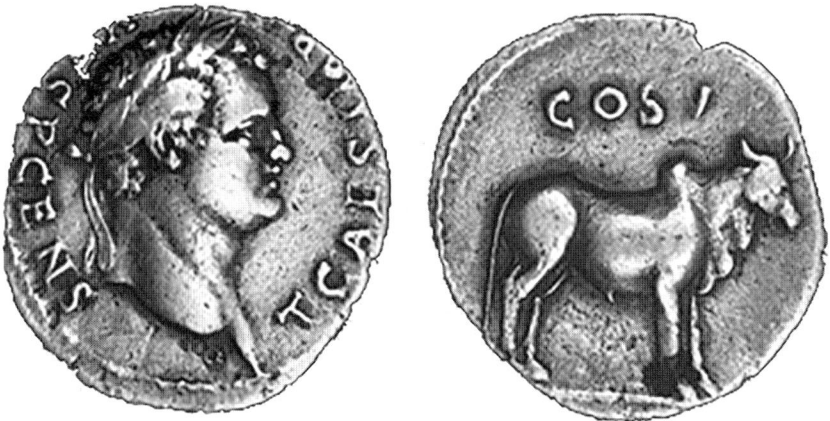

Silver Denarius of Titus.

associated to power with their father when the latter became emperor in 69. Titus is undoubtedly better recognized as the hero of the Judean War which began under *Nero* and which ended in 70 with the fall of Jerusalem. Between 71 and his own ascent to the purple cloak in 79, Titus was perceived as the unpopular heir, because as the head of the Praetorians, he performed unsightly tasks on behalf of his father such as the 'elimination' of certain troublesome political opponents.

When *Vespasian* died in 79, the question of succession posed no difficulties. Already associated to power, Titus replaced his father at the age of 40 and kept his younger brother *Domitian* near him even if there were tensions between the two

Statue of Titus in Delphi.

brothers. Titus proved very competent as an emperor. Having learned to govern with his father, he continued in the same direction. His very liberal reign was marked by extensive construction. In addition to erecting public buildings and continuing the construction of the Colosseum, he also extended the road infrastructure of the Empire. From a military point of view, the only significant event took place in Britannia, where the conquest of Caledonia (modern Scotland) was progressing. The reign of Titus was also marked by calamities. On 24 August, 79, a major eruption of Vesuvius buried Pompeii, Herculaneum and Stabies. A great fire ravaged Rome again in 80 and instigated an epidemic. In parallel with State agencies, the paternalistic emperor worked personally to relieve the victims with his own financial resources. Thanks to this kind of activity, which Titus performed frequently, his 26-month reign was enough to build a legendary reputation for kindness.

The reign of Titus, characterized by continuity, suddenly ended in 81. In circumstances similar to the death of *Vespasian* three years earlier, the death of Titus was probably linked to the abuse of the cold baths of Aquae Cutiliae despite some later rumours suggesting poisoning by his brother *Domitian*.

Domitian *Titus Flavius Domitianus*

Rome, Italy 51 – Rome, Italy 96
Reign: 81–96

Kept away from important decisions by his father *Vespasian* and then by his brother *Titus*, Domitian, once in power, imposed an absolutist-type of authority. He openly expressed indifference toward the Senate, which he perceived as a symbolic and obsolete figure of authority.

A competent man, Domitian practised internal and external policies generally in continuity with those of the first *Flavians*. He pursued the Roman 'universalization' of the socio-political institutions of the Empire. The era of conquest was coming to an end; stabilization and consolidation of the Empire's borders were now taking priority. A good administrator, undoubtedly his greatest quality as an emperor, and taking good care of the finances of the State, Domitian initiated reforms in this area hitherto fundamentally fuelled by the income generated by looting during

Silver Denarius of Domitian.

military operations. The good initial state of public finances allowed Domitian to carry out many architectural achievements and restoration projects in Rome and to build new roads in the outlying provinces of the Empire. Continuously working to please public opinion, Domitian was generous with the plebs, for whom he organized games and extravagances comparable to those in the time of *Nero*, and especially with the army, which received the first increase in pay since *Augustus*. These staggering expenses gradually drained the coffers of the State, and it is then that began the rise in taxes and the confiscation of property of senators who were too openly opposed to the type of Domitian absolutist authority.

From a military point of view, Domitian instigated expeditions against the Sarmatians and in Africa. He continued the pacification of northern Britannia but ended the incursions into Caledonia (modern Scotland), thus putting an end to attempts in conquering the Highlands. The most significant military theatre was on the Danube, embodied with punitive military expeditions against Germanic tribes and against a new threat to the Empire: the Dacians who were making incursions on Roman soil. Domitian himself participated in some of these expeditions. He completed the annexation of the Decumatian Fields (a territory of strategic defence between the Rhine and the Upper Danube) and erected the first fortified foundations of the *limes* on the Danube border.

While much appreciated by the plebeians and especially by the army, Domitian was hated by the aristocracy and the Senate, which he himself despised. His absolutist attitude, his austere financial measures and his persecuting actions perpetrated even against those close to him who were provoked by his unhealthy anxiety concerning his personal security made him powerful enemies. When the Praetorian Guard joined the ranks of his opponents, the inevitable happened. Under the tacit approval of the Praetorians and the Senate, the emperor's own servants who feared for their own lives murdered him in September 96. Domitian was 45 years old.

Nerva *Marcus Cocceius*

Narnia (Narni), Italy 30 – Rome, Italy 98
Reign: 96–98

As a member of a noble family from central Italy, Nerva's kinfolk had been in the imperial entourage since the time of *Tiberius*. In 71, Nerva was the only unrelated collaborator of *Vespasian*, usually assisted only by his sons *Titus* and *Domitian*. He became consul jointly with *Domitian* in 90 and then went into exile when *Domitian*'s persecutions against the aristocracy intensified. After the assassination of *Domitian* by his own servants in 96, the Senate chose Nerva as emperor.

The founder of the *Antonine* dynasty was a balanced, moderate, eloquent and very cultivated man. His liberal spirit reassured the aristocracy and the Senate, hard hit by *Domitian*, which wished to preserve the stable social climate bequeathed by the first *Flavians*. Nerva saw to a continuity in the administration and the finances, whose general state was still recoverable in spite of the disproportionate expenses of *Domitian*. He also practised a policy of collaboration with the Senate. Considerable resources were invested in public works and the road network in Italy. Nerva completed many construction projects undertaken under *Domitian*, many of which were quite advanced. During Nerva's reign, there was a markedly increased influence of the provincial aristocracy in State affairs through its ever-growing

Gold Aureus of Nerva.

presence in the Senate. The leadership of the Empire was no longer reserved for the Italian elite.

Having never held a military position, Nerva had no enemies in the military. This fact had a second impact: He also had no allies within the army. Consequently, the army displayed a generally neutral attitude toward the new emperor and in fact, part of the army still cherished the memory of *Domitian*, the first emperor since *Augustus* to have increased their pay.

Nerva was no more unanimous among the Praetorians. A political crisis threatened the stability of the reign, and the eventual succession of the 67-year-old emperor became a concern. Having no children, Nerva eased the agitation of the Praetorians by adopting *Trajan*, the governor of Upper Germania, in 97. Adopted by choice or under pressure, *Trajan*, who originated from Hispania (modern Spain) was designated as a successor. The choice of *Nerva* was wise, because by preferring to focus on merit rather than on a personal bond or on the origin of the candidate, it ensured the prosperity of the Empire. The plan was to place at the head of the Empire a competent man who was respected by both the military and the people. After having reigned only sixteen months, Nerva died of natural causes in 98 even before *Trajan* arrived in Rome.

Trajan *Marcus Ulpius Traianus*

Italica (near Seville), Spain 53 – Selinus (Musa Çay), Cilicia, Turkey 117
Reign: 98–117

Son of the governor of Syria, Trajan fought the Parthians under *Vespasian*. When *Nerva* became emperor in 96, Trajan was appointed governor of Upper Germania after leading a distinguished career in the army. Emperor *Nerva* adopted Trajan in 97 with the aim of restoring order in Rome, where the Praetorians were becoming restless. Once assured of his future accession, Trajan used a pretext to invite the insurgent Praetorian leaders to visit him in Germania in order to have them executed. The adoption of Trajan and the disappearance of the insurgent leaders were sufficient to restore order to Rome. When *Nerva* died the following year, Trajan became

Gold Aureus of Trajan.

the first non-Italian emperor in Roman history. Very capable, this emperor originating from Hispania (modern Spain) governed in collaboration with the Senate and was an excellent administrator and a great builder. Resisting the temptations of excess, his moderation ensured the continuity inherited from the *Flavians*, also preserved by its predecessor. Construction projects, motivated for practicability and not by personal extravagance, could be seen throughout the Empire. In Rome, the traces of the terrible fires of 64 and 80 disappeared. Following a design previously imagined by *Nerva*, Trajan set in motion an impressive social achievement for the time. The emperor decided to devote imperial funds to a special programme which aimed to feed the urban poor, a system that remained in place for two centuries.

It is under Trajan that the last two large scale military expeditions in Roman history took place. Since the reign of *Domitian*, the powerful Dacian kingdom posed a real threat beyond the *limes* of the Danube. *Domitian*, with partial military victories, somehow succeeded in repelling the Dacians and extracting a peace treaty from them. Around the year 100, the Dacians violated this treaty by resuming their raids inside the Empire. Trajan decided to put an end to this threat by invading and annexing the powerful Dacian kingdom. Following two laborious campaigns in 101 and 106, Trajan, on the border of the Danube, ensured an important complement to the defensive system of the region. In 113, Trajan undertook new successful major campaigns,

Trajan's Column in Rome.

this time against the Parthians. The result was the creation of two new provinces: Mesopotamia and Armenia. Even if Rome eventually evacuated the majority of these newly conquered eastern territories, Trajan ensured for the time better security for the trade routes in this region and reduced the permanent threat the Parthians had represented for more than a century against the provinces of the Orient. Under Trajan, the Empire reached its maximum geographic extent. Its vastness was already making it difficult to govern and to defend with the infrastructure and technological means of the time.

Trajan's reign was also significant socially. This period corresponded to the completion of the process of attaining social equilibrium in the Empire and of the *Pax romana*. In addition to having achieved political universalism and relative social homogeneity, Roman society reached a very high level of civilization. On the eve of his death in 117, Trajan, then aged 64, adopted his closest collaborator, *Hadrian*, who succeeded him.

Hadrian *Publius Aelius Hadrianus*

Italica (Santiponce), Spain 76 – Baiae (Bacoli), Italy 138
Reign: 117–138

Originating from a Picenian family of the Marche region of Italy who emigrated to Spain after the Punic Wars, Hadrian was part of the aristocracy. At the age of 10, he lost his father and henceforth became the protégé of *Trajan*, who was his father's cousin. After living a distracted youth, Hadrian, no doubt tutored by *Trajan*, began a military career. Military tribune in Lower Germania under *Domitian*, then governor of Lower Pannonia under *Trajan*, Hadrian participated alongside *Trajan* in the campaigns against the Dacians (101 and 107) and the Parthians (113–117) during which he was appointed governor of Syria. Well-prepared for political life by *Trajan*, whom he had accompanied since the beginning of his Principate, Hadrian was adopted by him on his deathbed in 117.

Hadrian was a very cultivated and fundamentally peaceful man. The writers and philosophers of his time found in this patron of Hellenic culture a competent critic. As a moderate, he applied an imperial policy

Silver Denarius of Hadrian.

falling within the framework of the continuity engendered by the *Flavians* and pursued by the first *Antonines*. He succeeded in achieving his political and social goals without undermining the financial and social balance of the Empire. The first achievements of his reign included fortifying the border with Mesopotamia and Armenia which he had evacuated, and repelling Sarmatian attacks in Dacia. Hadrian's ultimate goal was to preserve the perpetuity of the Empire by safeguarding its borders and keeping the peace within them. The era of great conquests

Statue of Hadrian in Delphi.

was definitely over. The legions, whose members had a deep affection for Hadrian, started to become solidly linked to the provinces in which they were stationed. Recruitment took place in the area, and soldiers maintained roads and bridges there.

There were two particularities to Hadrian's reign. The first was his personal inspection of the provinces and legions of the Empire. During these journeys, which lasted twelve years, the emperor fortified the *limes* and improved the discipline of the troops, while acquiring practical knowledge of the different regions of the Empire. The second was the development of the Perpetual Edict in 131. This document recorded the detailed standardization of the Roman code: legal proceedings, laws, rules of good citizenship, etc. Hadrian demonstrated his intention to continue standardization in the Empire. In fact, during his reign, the primacy of Italy over the provinces on the political scene, a state of affairs inherited from the time of the Republic, was almost entirely erased. This situation was mainly the result of the predominant presence of the provincial aristocracy in Rome, the widening of access to Roman citizenship and the universalization of social institutions. The *Pax romana* was at its pinnacle.

After his travels and having put down the last great Jewish revolt in 135, Hadrian's health began to deteriorate. His already obstinate character became predominant and he began to be suspicious of those around him. Yet only his collaborators and those close to him suffered the consequences of his sudden outbursts. Even though he became unpopular at the end of his life, Hadrian is today perceived positively as an emperor. Reign stability, prosperity as well as the social and financial equilibrium of the Empire were preserved.

Having no children, as *Nerva* and *Trajan* did before him, Hadrian preferred merit over family in choosing a successor. He therefore adopted *Antoninus* in 138. Shortly thereafter, at the age of 62, long-suffering Hadrian died in the presence of his successor.

Antoninus Pius *Titus Aelius Hadrianus Antoninus Pius*

Lanuvium (Lanuvio) Italy 86 – Lorium (near Castel di Guido), Italy 161
Reign: 138–161

Originating from an aristocratic Narbonne family, Antoninus was adopted by *Hadrian* in 138. He was then governor of Asia and 51 years old. *Hadrian*'s death came a few months after the adoption, and the succession went smoothly. This extremely wealthy career civil servant had never exercised military command. He continued the trend of collaboration with the Senate and of the rigorous administration of State affairs. Under *Trajan* and *Hadrian*, the imperial administrative

Silver Denarius of Antoninus Pius.

structures had reached their final forms. Antoninus had no excessive personal ambitions. He strengthened the application of administrative rules and laws in addition to fleshing out content in order to increase efficiency and eliminate loopholes that could have caused litigation in proceedings. Similar controls were also rigorously applied to State finances. Construction, although abundant, was generally limited to the restoration of existing structures. A policy of reducing imperial spending affected public activities. There was even a maximum limit for State grants, imposed by imperial decree, for games and celebrations for the people. That didn't refrain the celebrations of Rome's 900th anniversary from being impressive. In addition, the emperor still managed to establish and subsidize the Athenian schools, the ancestors of our modern universities.

Like those of his predecessors, Antoninus's main programme was aimed at preserving the military status quo. In the span of a generation, the concept of war of conquest had turned into a permanent and stationary effort for border protection. There was therefore very little military activity outside the borders apart from a temporary invasion of the south of Caledonia (modern Scotland). The wars of conquest were over, but the army remained formidable and suppressed any revolt and external incursion into Roman territory with prodigious efficiency. A new phenomenon, which was to become increasingly important, appeared in the Roman army: it was becoming increasingly difficult to recruit Roman citizens. For them, the military profession, stripped of any possibility of conquest, and therefore of the accumulation of spoils of war, lost part of its appeal. The authorities therefore turned to non-citizens and foreigners to fill the ranks of the legions. Even if we could not yet speak of the 'Germanization' of the Roman army, such elements were beginning to be visible within the ranks.

Antoninus's reign marked the height of the Empire. Social and financial equilibrium persisted, borders were well guarded, and the cultural influence of the Roman world radiated as far as India. A revival of religious fervour also marked this period of prosperity. Despite a Principate characterized by tolerance, Christianity began to seriously worry the elite because of its universal nature, which was directly in conflict with the worship of the imperial deity.

Following a brief illness, Antoninus died in 161 at the age of 75. By his kindness and moderation, he had attracted the sympathy and respect of all. His adopted son *Marcus Aurelius*, whom he adopted when he was himself adopted by *Hadrian* in 138, succeeded him.

Marcus Aurelius *Marcus Aelius Aurelius Verus*

Rome, Italy 121 – Vindobona (Vienna), Austria 180
Reign: 161–180

Marcus Aurelius and *Lucius Verus* were adopted by *Antoninus* in 138. In 161, Marcus succeeded him as emperor. He renewed the system of co-regency by immediately associating himself with his adopted brother *Lucius Verus*. History recalls that Marcus was a philosopher who was also cultivated, tolerant, modest and conservative. The new 40-year-old emperor was a frail-looking man with great intelligence. He had experienced power because at a young age he had assisted *Antoninus* while the latter was emperor. In addition to strengthening the administrative centralization of the Empire in Rome, he pursued the tradition of collaboration with the Senate and the aristocracy.

Following a prosperous and rather quiet period under the reign of *Antoninus*, a troubled era began to shake up the Empire. In addition to three major military campaigns which, for the first time, severely tested the defence structure of the Empire, a plague and a subsequent

Silver Denarius of Marcus Aurelius.

Statue of Marcus
Aurelius in Rome.

famine disrupted the social and financial equilibrium of the Roman
world. Barely having donned the imperial purple cloak, Marcus faced
his first showdown when the Parthians invaded Armenia. *Lucius
Verus* successfully led the campaign in the East (161–166). As soon as
the victory festivities ended, the Germanic tribes of the Marcomanni
and the Quadi crossed the Danubian border. With two harsh military
campaigns (168–175 and 178–180), Marcus, now alone following the
death of *Lucius Verus* in 169, succeeded in pushing the Germanic
invaders back behind the *limes* and securing the borders of the Empire.

Marcus's domestic activities were relatively few since war occupied
most of his reign. There was little money left in the coffers for
construction because of the heavy expenses associated with military

expeditions and the significant decrease in the inflows of money due to the plague and famine. In fact, construction was limited to restoring and strengthening the fortifications of border towns. Despite this restrictive financial situation, Marcus continued to grant subsidies to the Athenian schools, ancestors of our modern universities, and organized public activities such as circus games, despite his personal disdain for this type of spectacle.

However, despite being a generally tolerant man, Marcus stood firm against the Christians whose numbers were constantly growing. The universalist concept linked to the Church contrasted with that of the Empire. Christians were seen as members of a parallel authority that was opposed to that of the emperor. What made the emperor philosopher suspicious of Christians was the apparent fanaticism with which many of them voluntarily submitted to the worst sufferings in the name of their faith. The primacy of the bishop of Rome timidly began to stand out from the other bishops of the Empire, this was the birth of the papal concept. The first persecutions, although sporadic, began their sinister fame.

Following the revolt of a usurper in the East, previously one of the most loyal generals to the emperor, Marcus proclaimed his son *Commodus* co-emperor and heir to prevent the recurrence of such a situation. During the second campaign on the Danube (178–180), accompanied by *Commodus*, Marcus who was about to fully take advantage of his recent victory against the Germanic invaders, but who had been ill for some time, died in the Vindobona legionnaire camp (modern Vienna).

Lucius Verus *Lucius Aelius Aurelius Commodus*

Rome, Italy 130 – Altinum (now part of Venice), Italy 169
Reign: 161–169
When *Hadrian* adopted *Antoninus* in 138, *Antoninus* at the same time adopted *Marcus Aurelius*, 17 years old and Lucius Verus, 7 years old. On the death of *Antoninus* in 161, *Marcus Aurelius* succeeded him as emperor and immediately associated himself with his adopted brother Lucius. By doing so, *Marcus Aurelius* introduced the system of co-

Silver Denarius of Lucius Verus.

regency even if in reality, he controlled the levers of power. In order to strengthen the family ties between the two men, *Marcus Aurelius* offered his daughter Lucilla, then 12 years old, in marriage to Lucius. Although he boasted a strong and vigorous physique, Lucius wasn't suited to lead the Empire. A sportsman avid for the pleasures of life, he seemed to be an honest and just man, but had no interest in politics or in State affairs. Satisfied to follow the instructions of *Marcus Aurelius*, Lucius with his courageous and adventurous character turned out to be a capable military leader. He quickly had the opportunity to shine in 161, when the Parthians crossed the eastern border and invaded Armenia. The succession being too recent, *Marcus Aurelius* wished to avoid that the two emperors leave Rome at the same time, so he instructed his brother to personally direct the war against the Parthians. While the eastern provinces were being attacked, Lucius's journey eastbound was unhurried. He lingered in Greece, where he was seduced by multiple distractions and undoubtedly by some bacchanalia. Ultimately, he arrived in the East where his generals led a victorious campaign against the Parthian invaders (161–166). During this campaign, a plague afflicting the Parthian armies appeared in the ranks of the legions. After Lucius's equally long journey back to Rome, victory was celebrated while the plague was spreading and began to decimate the population across the Empire.

In 168, a Germanic coalition made up of the Marcomanni and the Quadi launched a coordinated attack and pierced the defensive *limes* on the Danubian border. They managed to reach northern Italy before a Roman counter-offensive was launched. The two brothers jointly started the campaign, but almost immediately, Lucius, now sick, turned back leaving *Marcus Aurelius* to continue alone. On the way back to Rome, Lucius died. He was 38.

Commodus *Lucius Aurelius Commodus*

Lanuvium (Lanuvio), Italy 161 – Rome, Italy 192)
Reign: 180–192

Despite rumours that suggested his father was a gladiator, Commodus was most likely the legitimate son of *Marcus Aurelius* with whom he was associated to power in 177. During the second major campaign against the Germanic tribes on the Danube border in 180, *Marcus Aurelius* died and Commodus, then 19 years old, succeeded him as the head of the Empire. The new Principate began with positivism, because the young emperor, with his intelligence, his apparent moderation and his athletic physique, seemed predisposed to assume his sacred role well. In addition, Commodus was well surrounded by his father's advisors. However, just like his uncle *Lucius Verus*, co-emperor and adopted brother of *Marcus Aurelius*, Commodus had no sense of duty and quickly lost interest in politics. Soon demonstrating

Silver Denarius of Commodus.

trends of megalomania, Commodus preferred to take advantage of the privileges linked to his social position and to give himself up to the pleasures of life and the circus games by sometimes participating in them himself. Until 182, the reign was stable. The emperor's competent advisors led the Empire while Commodus, indifferent, sank into debauchery. Following attacks on his life, Commodus's advisors were gradually replaced by ambitious individuals more concerned with their own interests than with the salvation of the Empire. Difficulties soon arose in internal affairs. The administration became mired in corruption, and the finances were hard hit by the staggering expenses related to the festivities and games during which extravagance was in order. Persecution against the Senate and the aristocracy resumed, breaking a century of social harmony among the Roman elite.

Despite the commotions taking place in Rome, external affairs were generally stable. With the exception of the incursions of the Brigantes into northern Britannia, the border situation was calm. In general, the governors managed their province adequately and the legions remained at their posts. By this time, the enrolment of Germanic elements in the Roman army was common. Fortunately, the rapid 'Romanization' of their ever-increasing numbers avoided potential problems of discipline, cohesion and allegiance.

As for religion, Commodus's admiration for the mysticism and esotericism of the eastern cults was responsible for his indifference toward Christians. For a while, imperial persecution ceased, and Christians enjoyed relative freedom.

In 190, the debauched life of Commodus reached a sinister summit. Never before had the Empire been led by such a disgraceful character. Probably mad, he identified himself with the god Hercules and tried to imitate him in every way imaginable. His indolence at the beginning of the reign turned into an attitude of suspicion and the attacks against the aristocracy were accentuated. Now no senator was untouchable. In December 192, on the eve of grandiose games, he was strangled after a failed poisoning attempt. It would therefore be said of him that he was crueler than *Domitian* and madder than *Nero*.

Pertinax *Publius Helvius*

Alba Pompeia (Alba), Italy 126 – Rome, Italy 193
Reign: 193

Pertinax originated from the most modest class of Roman society; once a slave, his father became successful in trade. Pertinax rose to the top of the hierarchy of the Roman world by his own means and wit. With a good education in his back pocket, Pertinax began a military career at the age of 35. During *Lucius Verus*'s campaign against the Parthians (161–166), he distinguished himself in combat during his command of a Gallic cohort of approximately 500 men. He was then quickly promoted to tribune of the sixth legion stationed in Britannia. He participated in the harsh campaigns of *Marcus Aurelius* against Germanic tribes (168–180). As a reward for his services, he was appointed senator and then governor of Syria in 180. Under the reign of *Commodus*, he was also well appreciated. In 189 he was appointed prefect of Rome, a position he still held when *Commodus* was assassinated. Elected emperor by the assassins of *Commodus*, Pertinax, aged 66, accepted his new role following the approval of the Senate and, of course, after having paid the traditional liberality to the Praetorians. The new emperor restored the practice of the reign in collaboration with the Senate in addition to carrying out legal reforms concerning the legislation of personal wills. The dismal State finances demanded the strengthening of a strict economy. Out of

Silver Denarius of Pertinax.

ordinary tax earnings on one hand, including income from the sale of *Commodus*'s properties and possessions, and the reduction in expenses on the other, it became possible to meet essential needs such as the food supply of the capital and the minimum maintenance of its public buildings and surrounding roads.

Pertinax was an honest and well-intended man, but he made the mistake of trying to change too many things too quickly. He was strict on the military, especially the Praetorians. More accustomed to extravagance and carelessness than to training under *Commodus*, the Praetorians quickly withdrew their support for the emperor when he tried to subject them to a more vigorous and stricter military discipline. By accusing them of fraud, the emperor also cracked down on the corrupt, freed and opportunist slaves who, under *Commodus*, had taken over the key posts of imperial offices. The people were delighted with these restrictive measures against the Praetorians and vile officials, but Pertinax had put himself in a precarious position by alienating important support for his authority.

Following two failures of the Praetorians to have the emperor replaced by another suitor they had chosen, the guard took up arms and revolted. Several hundred Praetorian soldiers stormed the imperial palace without the guards or the officials even thinking of resisting. Refusing to flee, Pertinax decided to meet the mutineers to try to reason with them. While the emperor was discussing with the mob, an enraged soldier rushed out of the ranks and stabbed him. Despite the short duration of Pertinax's reign, barely three months, he had earned the respect of the Senate and of the people.

Didius Julianus *Marcus Didius Severus Julianus*

Mediolanum (Milan), Italy 133 – Rome, Italy 193
Reign: 193
A senior civil servant in the administration who also had experience in military life, Senator Didius Julianus was part of the entourage of Emperor *Marcus Aurelius*. It was therefore under the aegis of this imperial family that he pursued a very lucrative career. Governor in Belgium and then in Germania, he repelled incursions of the

Gold Aureus of Didius Julianus.

Germanic Chauci and Chatti on the banks of the Elbe River. In 176, under *Marcus Aurelius*, he was appointed proconsul of the province of Africa following the promotion of the future emperor *Pertinax* who previously held the position.

Immediately following the assassination of *Pertinax*, the Praetorians took refuge in their fortified barracks in Rome, la Castra Praetoria, fearing a popular revolt. It was then that an unexpected scene took place there and that the sacred role of emperor was adjudicated to the richest bidder. It was of course the question of the size of the dowry paid to the Praetorians. Two suitors coveted the post: Flavius Sulpicianus, a relative of *Pertinax*, and senior imperial official Didius Julianus. Offers were exchanged until Didius's impressive wealth proved him right over his rival. He was then immediately proclaimed emperor by the Praetorians. The Senate, recalcitrant, but faced with a fait accompli, confirmed him in his new functions. The people remained hostile to this unusual appointment, and a show of force was necessary on the part of Didius to confirm his fragile authority. Most historians agree that despite the fact that he was designated emperor in an atypical way, Didius was a natural candidate for the task.

Didius's reign began badly. To the insecurity caused by the hostility of the people was added the distrust of the Senate and a rebellion in the army, which was exasperated by the privileges reserved for Praetorians, including by their role in making and defeating emperors. The army of the East named its own emperor in the person of Pescennius Niger, governor of Syria. The legions of Britannia also appointed one of their own as emperor, the governor of Britannia Clodius Albinus. Finally, the Danube army also chose an emperor in the person of the governor of Pannonia, *Septimius Severus*. A cunning man, the latter knew that everything was decided in Rome. So, he took the initiative by buying the neutrality of Clodius Albinus and outstripping his most formidable competitor, Pescennius Niger, by invading Italy and marching against Didius. Didius's situation was now hopeless. Following attempts to have Pescennius Niger and *Septimius Severus* assassinated, the emperor attempted to organize the defence of Italy. He only had a few detachments of local garrisons at his disposal: gladiators and the Praetorians, who were much less resilient than their predecessors a century and a half previous. In fact, softened by its prolonged contact with routine activity and with the idleness linked to the luxury of urban life in the capital, the Praetorian Guard was no longer the elite combat unit of yesteryear.

The meagre troops sent to fight *Septimius Severus* in fact joined his army. To unify the soldiers, *Septimius Severus* used the memory of *Pertinax*, made popular by his victories against the Barbarians. Very skilfully, he let the Praetorians know that he would spare them if they brought him *Pertinax*'s assassins. Realizing that their situation was hopeless and fearing for their lives, the Praetorians accepted the ultimatum. Upon receiving the news, the Senate voted the forfeiture of Didius, who, alone and abandoned by all, was assassinated. His reign lasted only sixty-six days, yet he did not deserve his sinister fate any more than anyone else.

Septimius Severus *Licius Septimius Severus*

Leptis Magna (near Khoms), Libya 146 – Eboracum (York), England 211
Reign: 193–211

When *Pertinax* was assassinated in 193, *Didius Julianus* was appointed emperor in particular circumstances, the sacred role of emperor being adjudicated to the highest bidder. Three governors acclaimed as emperors by their own armies rejected the nomination of *Didius*

Silver coin of Septimius Severus.

Julianus. One of them, Septimius Severus, who was ahead of the other two competitors, immediately made his way to Rome with an army to face *Didius Julianus.* Once the latter was defeated and then assassinated, a new turbulent reign began. Septimius's career path did not differ greatly from those of his predecessors. The first emperor born in Africa was a member of the equestrian order when he was admitted to the senatorial order by *Marcus Aurelius.* Proconsul of Africa in 174, he then became proconsul of Sicily in 189, and then governor of Pannonia under *Commodus.*

Once donning the purple cloak, Septimius retracted his promise not to crack down on the Praetorians who remained loyal to *Didius Julianus* and followed *Vitellius*'s example of 124 years before. After executing those who had assassinated *Pertinax,* Septimius dissolved the Praetorian Guard and dispersed its former members to reconstitute it immediately with members of his own army. From that point on, access to this elite corps, previously reserved almost exclusively for Italian soldiers, was extended to provincial soldiers. An intelligent administrator, possibly tinged with a taste for literature and philosophy, Septimius was better recognized for his spitefulness and for his reign as an absolute monarch. His obstinacy in reigning without sharing power made him a persecutor of the aristocracy and the Senate from which he wrested the last bits of authority.

The first part of Septimius's reign boiled down to the consolidation of his authority and then of the eastern border of the Empire. After a fifteen-month struggle, he succeeded in eliminating the threat of the pretender to the purple cloak, the governor of Syria, Pescennius Niger, at the Battle of Issus in 194. Two years later, the second pretender, the governor of Britannia, Clodius Albius, renounced his neutrality, or was forced to do so by his own troops, and opposed Severus. The latter defeated Clodius Albius at the Battle of Lyon in 197. The wars of consolidation barely over, Septimius had to return to the East in order to keep in check the Parthians, who were again becoming agitated at the border. The emperor remained there until 199 to straighten the defensive system of the region and to secure the loyalty of the provinces that had been loyal to Pescennius Niger. The founder of the *Severan* dynasty began to properly reign in 202. Now that peace had returned, Septimius proceeded to reform Roman law in order to make it more accessible and less rigid. He restored a certain balance in the imperial budget despite the expenses due to the long wars, to new constructions and to the 'deficit' inherited from *Commodus*. The imperial finances were straightened out thanks to wise administration, to the entry of new sums generated by the confiscation of the goods of Albius and Niger, and to the booty accumulated during the campaign against the Parthians.

From a military point of view, the emperor of African origin was making changes. At the beginning of the third century, the Germanic barbarians seemed less threatening than the Parthians. Certain legions were therefore relocated to the East, thus stripping the *limes* of the Rhine. For the first time in the history of the Empire, a legion was permanently stationed in Italy. The emperor had feared the same fate that many of his predecessors have suffered. Indeed, faced with an invasion of Italy by a contender for the purple cloak, many emperors found themselves defenceless in Rome.

Septimius repeated to his sons, whom he had associated to power, that the soldiers had to be well-taken care of, whatever the cost. In that vein, the condition of the legionary was enhanced during his reign. Reigning as an absolute monarch, Severus ensured the loyalty of the army on which his authority rested entirely. Salaries and privileges for soldiers were increased, and soldiers could now marry and start families during military service. Permanent settlements then began to form around the legionary camps all along the frontier (*limes*) from which many future European capitals would emerge.

In 211, Septimius, who was waging war in the north of Britannia in Scotland, suddenly fell ill and died. He left the Empire to his two sons, who hated each other and who decided to abandon the military campaign immediately.

During his turbulent eighteen-year reign, Septimius managed to restore finances and erase the apparent traces of the depraved reign of *Commodus*. However, the Empire was about to embark on a path of a long and gradual decline. The economic balance of the Empire, which had been established by the *Julio-Claudians*, maintained by the *Flavians*, and reached full maturity under the *Antonines*, was now in a precarious state.

Geta *Publius Septimius*

Rome, Italy 189 – Rome, Italy 211
Reign: 211
When *Septimius Severus* died in northern Britannia during a military campaign in Caledonia (Scotland), in 211, his two sons, *Caracalla* and Geta, who had already been appointed to succeed him, became co-emperors. Raised under the title of *Caesar* in 198 then of *Augustus*

Gold Aureus of Geta.

in 209, Geta, who was endowed with a high level of intelligence, was much less rustic in behaviour and appearance than his brother *Caracalla*. The latter had the primacy of power, but the support of the powerful empress mother Julia Domna in favour of Geta forced *Caracalla* to share power. Once the honours were delivered to their deceased father, the animosity between the two brothers was unleashed. They even had planned to divide the Empire, the East for Geta and the West for *Caracalla*, but the opposition of their mother Julia Domna forced the abandonment of this project, which under these conditions would likely have degenerated into a civil war. The hatred that persisted between the brothers pushed *Caracalla* to the extreme. Not wanting to face Geta openly because of the support he had within the aristocracy, he schemed to get rid of him. On the pretext of a false plot to assassinate the two brothers, Geta was killed while *Caracalla* claimed to have escaped his attackers. Geta was 23. The dualist reign that *Septimius Severus* had wished harmonious between his two sons ended in bloodshed, ten months following his death.

Caracalla *Lucius Septimius Bassianus*

Lugdunum (Lyon), France 188 – Carrhes (Harran), Turkey 217
Reign: 211–217

When *Septimius Severus* died in 211, power was shared between his two sons, Bassianus and *Geta*. Ten months later, hatred drove Bassianus to have his brother killed. Bassianus, more remembered by his nickname of Caracalla because of the long coat he liked to wear (caracallus), made a generous distribution of money to the Praetorians and wheat to the people in order to prevent an organized reaction by the supporters of *Geta*, whose leaders were in turn assassinated. According to many historians, Caracalla lived an exemplary childhood, and it was later that he was drawn into a fierce rivalry with his brother *Geta*. His character eventually hardened to the point of making him sickly, insecure and cruel.

Under the pretext of avoiding plots against him, the emperor got rid of potential and imaginary rivals and filled the State coffers with

Silver Antoninianus of Caracalla.

the goods of his generally innocent victims. The new 24-year-old emperor confiscated and ordered arbitrary assassinations during his entire reign. Caracalla, a brutal and physically ugly man, fought more violently than his father against the aristocracy and the Senate. He was also mainly concerned with the army. In fact, military activity was his only interest, which is why he left it to his mother, Julia Domna, to manage the affairs of the Empire. The internal achievements of his reign were thus made possible thanks to the intervention of his mother and the advisors around him.

The highlight of the reign was undoubtedly the edict of Caracalla in 212. Despite the many restrictions and the limited extent of its immediate impact, the edict extended access to Roman citizenship to most of the inhabitants of the Empire. Of course, the main motivation behind the establishment of the edict was more financial than humanistic: it aimed to stimulate the flow of capital. More significantly, the increase in the number of citizens also implied a growth in State revenues through the numerous taxes reserved for this social class. It should be noted on the one hand that the inheritance tax, among Roman citizens, was increased from five to ten per cent shortly before the edict came into effect. On the other hand, the more extensible access and the growing economic disadvantages linked to the title was to cause a decrease in the prestige linked to Roman citizenship in the long term, which was to make it lose its appeal. One consequence of the edict was certain: the consolidation of the concept that the Empire had become a collective, a community. It was no longer just a simple amalgamation of territories ruled by Rome.

Like his father *Septimius Severus* before him, Caracalla worked to improve the condition of the soldiers. In addition to spending a lot of time with the military, he significantly increased their pay. This undoubtedly explained the popularity of Caracalla among the legions. Despite the military campaigns that were carried out, very few significant victories were acquired by force of arms. During a military campaign against the Parthians (214–217), the emperor's macabre reputation as 'arbitrary murderer' turned against him. The Praetorian prefect *Macrinus*, who accompanied Caracalla to the East, began to fear for his life when rumours started to surface suggesting that he was a rival to the emperor. *Macrinus* decided to act by having Caracalla secretly murdered by one of his own bodyguards.

Without the positive achievements of his mother Julia Domna surrounded by competent advisors, the reign of Caracalla would probably have been perceived as mediocre. Caracalla arbitrarily orchestrated numerous persecutions against the aristocracy, the Senate and the Christians. His conduct could place him in the same lineage of infamous characters such as *Caligula*, *Nero*, *Domitian* and *Commodus*.

Macrinus *Marcus Opellius Macrinus*

Caesarea (Cherchel), Algeria 164 – Archelais (Aksaray), Turkey 218 Reign: 217–218

Above all, history remembers Macrinus for his apparent appetite for opulence, which was perhaps exaggerated when compared to the financial rigidity practised by his two predecessors. This being said, he was quite knowledgeable in the legal and financial domains, which served to have him appointed director of the imperial post during the reign of *Septimius Severus*. In 212, *Caracalla* put him in charge of the prefecture of the courtroom. During a campaign against the Parthians, *Caracalla*, who arbitrarily eliminated anyone deemed threatening to his authority, began to suspect his lieutenant Macrinus. The latter,

Gold Aureus of Macrinus.

fearing for his life, decided to get ahead of the emperor and had him murdered. Because *Caracalla* had not yet prepared his succession, the generals of the eastern army, who seemed to ignore Macrinus's role in the assassination, immediately proclaimed him emperor. The Senate was relieved by the disappearance of *Caracalla* and confirmed the decision. However, a large part of the aristocracy was outraged to see a member of the equestrian order appropriating the purple cloak. Macrinus's advent as emperor had been an unforeseen event because neither his social status nor his origins had made him a likely successor to *Caracalla*. Furthermore, he was not related to the *Severans*.

Macrinus's political initiatives were at the very least unfortunate. In the area of external affairs, because Macrinus sought peace at all cost with the Parthians, he negotiated a dishonourable agreement following a battle with an uncertain outcome. His popularity with the army quickly disappeared after this failure. Internally, the situation was scarcely brighter. In addition to certain political blunders, there was growing opposition to his authority because of his modest and purely civil origin. His downfall took place when he announced a significant reduction in military spending, which the legionaries, pampered by the first two *Severans*, did not appreciate to say the least.

When part of the army of the East proclaimed the young *Elagabalus* emperor in Emesa (Homs), Macrinus tried to defeat this rival, who turned out to be *Caracalla*'s 14-year-old nephew. The first attack against *Elagabalus* failed, during which Macrinus lost his closest advisor, the courtroom prefect, in the fray. At this point, part of his own army abandoned him to join the ranks of the legitimate successor of the *Severan* dynasty, despite Macrinus's promise of a lucrative subsidy (*congiarium*) to the troops. The rest of his army was again beaten in Syria. This time, control over the East escaped him. In July 218, disguised as a soldier while trying to reach Rome to find support and rebuild an army, he was recognized by the soldiers, captured and killed. Unable to win a decisive victory over the Parthians and having reduced the privileges of the military, Macrinus's short reign was terminated, and the purple cloak returned to the *Severans*.

Elagabalus *Varius Avitus Bassianus*

Emesa (Homs), Syria 204 – Rome, Italy 222
Reign: 218–222

Nephew of *Caracalla*, this 14-year-old boy was already high priest of an oriental cult dedicated to Baal, the supreme solar god of Emesis, when he was elevated emperor by part of the army of the East. This achievement was carried out because of the skilful machinations of Elagabalus's grandmother, Julia Maesa, who was the sister of Julia Domna, wife of *Septimius Severus* and mother of *Caracalla*. Under the reign of this Syrian priest, Semitic cults, even Christians, were

Gold Aureus of Elagabalus.

allowed to practise freely. Carrying a popular nickname from the name of the god he served with such enthusiasm, Elagabalus was the living example, in appearance, of an oriental prince of the time. As an eccentric dresser, he boasted an almost erotic mysticism in his double role of emperor and high priest. He scandalized Rome when he entered it in 219, dressed as a Parthian prince. Elagabalus very early demonstrated the signs of mental imbalance that his premature elevation to boundless privileges, linked to absolute power, would continue to embolden. The depraved young adolescent quickly indulged in the most vicious abuses. Thus, added to the daily life of the emperor were sexual perversion and mystical madness related to the practice of his worship.

Elagabalus's young age and his compelling duty to serve Baal, who temporarily became the supreme god of the Roman world, left real power in the hands of Julia Maesa. The beginning of the reign was characterized by multiple executions of suspected pretenders to the purple cloak and in repression of civil riots. Once order was restored, the next three years boiled down to a political status quo. There were no military expeditions beyond the borders and no changes to the internal political scene except for the erection and restoration of some buildings. State mechanisms continued to operate on the strength of previous emperors.

The emperor's debauchery surpassed everything known until then. It ended up exhausting the resources of the imperial treasury, fuelled above all by the confiscation of property following the assassination of aristocrats with divergent opinions, ordered by the emperor or Julia Maesa. The reputation of Elagabalus and his mother spread quickly throughout the Empire. Along with the simmering revolt within the army, popular indignation set in. Under pressure from Julia Maesa, who was worried about the future, Elagabalus adopted his cousin *Severus Alexander* in 221 and appointed him as his successor. The emperor quickly regretted his decision because his enemies appreciated *Severus Alexander*. He therefore attempted to turn the Praetorians against him, but the plot turned against Elagabalus, and the exasperated Praetorians murdered him instead. The estranged and depraved oriental prince was only 18 years old.

Severus Alexander *Bassianus Alexianus*

Caesarea (Keisarya), Israel 208 – Moguntiacum (Mainz), Germany 235 Reign: 222–235.

After the fall of *Macrinus* in 219, Severus Alexander, then 10 years old, followed the new emperor, his cousin *Elagabalus*, to Rome. During this depraved reign, Severus's mother, Julia Mammaea, devoted herself to his education and saved him from the perverse influences of the court. Faced with the desire to preserve the purple cloak within the *Severan* family, *Elagabalus* was forced to adopt Severus in 221. Following the assassination of *Elagabalus* by the Praetorians, Severus was immediately proclaimed in his new position. The 14-year-old new emperor was still heavily influenced by his mother Julia Mammaea. At the beginning of the reign, she was the one who, surrounded by competent advisors and jurists, essentially ruled the Empire. Severus had personal virtues that contrasted greatly with the excesses of *Elagabalus*. Gifted with a high intellectual culture and moderation, he evoked the memory of *Marcus Aurelius*. With his type of authority, Severus did not manifest the absolutist tendencies of the other *Severans*. He reigned in collaboration with the Senate even if his decisions were often dictated by the will of his mother. A supporter of religious syncretism, he tolerated if not protected Christians. During his reign, administrative and legal reforms were

Silver Denarius of Severus Alexander.

carried out in favour of free men and slaves. Economic practices were simple and conservative without, however, being too rigid. In addition to restoring the Empire's public infrastructure, the emperor distributed meat to the people and financial support to rhetoricians, grammarians, doctors and architects. Even low interest loans were made to poor farmers.

The emperor's virtues and administrative skills made him popular with the people. However, his obvious lack of leadership and willpower in the face of thorny military issues offset his successes during this difficult period, when the loyalty of the army had become a crucial and fluctuating element. Numerous palace intrigues appeared under his very nose without the emperor intervening, and military seditions were frequent. Severus's two military campaigns highlighted these shortcomings. In 226, an important dynastic change at the head of the Parthian Empire shifted the balance of power in the East. In 231, the Parthians, henceforth known as the Persians, ravaged the eastern provinces of the Roman Empire. After failed attempts at negotiations with the Persians, Severus, conflicted, was forced to take up arms. Following an unsuccessful military campaign and heavy casualties, peace was temporarily restored in the region. This military failure was poorly digested by the soldiers, who believed they had been restrained from fighting by an early end to the hostilities. Faced with a new external threat, this time on the Germanic front in 234, the emperor tried to buy peace from the Germanic invaders at a high price instead of fighting them. This second incident caused the fall of Severus. The emperor's obvious subordination to his mother, the recent shameful stalemate against the Persians and finally this impression of submission to the Barbarians resulted in part of his army suppressing their loyalty toward him.

The soldiers, bitterly disappointed, then chose one of their generals to replace Severus. *Maximinus Thrax*, whose bravery in past wars had made him popular, was thus proclaimed emperor. Faced with this serious act, Severus again refused to take up arms and lead his army to defend his position, which had now become precarious. Faced with this demonstration of weakness, the troops that had remained loyal to him abandoned him. Shortly afterwards, Severus and his mother were assassinated by *Maximinus Thrax*'s men inside a legionnaire's camp. The reign of Severus is perceived by modern historians as an honourable one. Its administrative measures temporarily delayed the decline of the Roman political apparatus. But despite Severus's intelligence and personal virtues, it was his obvious lack of will that led to his fall.

Maximinus Thrax *Caius Julius Verus Maximinus*

Sopianae (Pécs), Hungary 173 – Aquileia, Italy 238
Reign: 235–238

This former Thracian shepherd, of reputedly imposing size, was an uneducated and boorish man but of undeniable bravery. This in addition to his physical strength were the source of his military fortune. In 191, under *Commodus*, Maximinus Thrax enlisted in the Thracian auxiliary cavalry to quickly climb the ranks. In 232, as prefect of Mesopotamia, he distinguished himself during the Persian War of *Severus Alexander*. When the campaign against the Alemanni was launched in 235, Maximinus directed the training of recruits. When the last *Severan* was assassinated that same year, the troops acclaimed him emperor. For the first time in the history of the Empire, a simple non-commissioned soldier, without a senatorial or equestrian title, acquired the purple cloak.

Gold Aureus of Maximinus I Thrax.

The beginning of the reign was marked by the failure of two assassination attempts against Maximinus. They came from the aristocracy and the Senate, who objected to seeing a character with modest origins and without education lead the Empire. Knowing the unconditional hostility of these two groups, Maximinus decided before returning to Rome to carry out a military campaign in order to gain the confidence of the people of the capital. The new emperor liberated the Decumatian Fields (area between the Rhine, Main, and Danube rivers of the Roman provinces of Germania Superior and Raetia), which the Alemanni had invaded, and pursued them deep into Germanic territory, where he severely beat them repeatedly despite heavy losses. This campaign was a feat in itself, as legions rarely ventured so deeply into hostile Germanic lands. In 236, he carried out a second campaign beyond the Danube and came out victorious over the Sarmatians. Despite these remarkable military successes, the popularity of Maximinus did not change. These expeditions and the reconstruction of the road network undertaken by the emperor were expensive. Maximinus had to increase the inflows of money in order to finance these expenses. The emperor first targeted the wealthiest of the wealthy with the help of informers and false trials, then drew on State funds reserved for the poor and for the capital's food supply. These austere measures increased the opposition of the owners, the aristocracy and now the less fortunate peasants.

In 238, a revolt erupted in the province of proconsular Africa under the aegis of the rich governor *Gordian I* and his son *Gordian II*, whom the insurgents designated co-emperors. The Senate then used the opportunity to raise Italy against Maximinus, who at the time was on the Germanic border. In the capital, the populace overthrew the statues of the emperor, and the prefect of the city as well as the prefect of the court were assassinated. The Praetorians who were supporting Maximinus were forced to stay in their barracks. The African revolt was quickly suppressed by the legion stationed there who had remained loyal to Maximinus. Following this event, the latter then decided to march on Italy. The Senate, now compromised, sprang into action. As a pardon from Maximinus did not seem to be conceivable, the Senate chose two new emperors from its own ranks, Senators *Pupienus* and

Balbinus. Before heading for Rome, Maximinus, with the help of his Pannonian army, laid siege to Aquileia, which refused to open its doors to the emperor's troops. The Senate also had the roads leading to Aquileia blocked in order to isolate Maximinus's army and to deprive it of food. The length of the siege and the lack of food among the besiegers exasperated the emperor, so he executed certain officers whom he considered incapable. The effect of these acts proved less than desirable for the emperor and further demotivated his soldiers to fight. A group of officers, now weary of fighting their compatriots, decided to murder Maximinus and his son, who had been named *Caesar* the year before.

Gordian I *Marcus Antonius Gordianus Sempronianus*

Phrygia region, Turkey 157 – Carthago (Tunis), Tunisia 238
Reign: 238

This senator of Anatolian origin, author of an account of thirty books on the lives of *Antoninus Pius* and *Marcus Aurelius*, was a cultivated man, honest and rich but without grandiose ambitions. Praetorian legate of lower Britannia in 216 under *Caracalla*, consul in 221 under *Elagabalus*, then governor of Africa in 235 under *Severus Alexander*, Gordian I was 80 years old when the events of 238 soared him to the purple cloak.

When a revolt was taken up by peasants and landlords in Africa, exasperated by the oppressive financial measures imposed on them

Sestertius of Gordian I.

by *Maximinus*, the insurgents proclaimed their governor as emperor. Gordian I, who at first hesitated, eventually yielded to pressure, accepted and associated his son *Gordian II* to power. When the news reached the Senate in Rome, the Gordians were immediately recognized, and *Maximinus* was declared a public enemy. Italy immediately rose against *Maximinus*. Even before the authority of the Gordians left Africa, its momentum was shattered by the army of the Numidian legate, who remained loyal to *Maximinus*. Legate Capellianus walked on Carthage, which had become the capital of the Gordians. The makeshift Gordian army led by *Gordian II* was massacred by the Legio III Augusta, and *Gordian II* was killed in the fray. Now realizing that he had lost his cause, Gordian I committed suicide before Carthage fell. So ended his reign of just four weeks. While Italy escaped from the control of *Maximinus*, Africa was brought back under his authority.

Gordian II *Marcus Antonius Gordianus Sempronianus Junior*

Place of birth unknown 192 – Carthago (Tunis), Tunisia 238
Reign: 238
Son of *Gordian I*, Gordian II was a cultivated and literate man. Quaestor under *Elagabalus* then consul under *Severus Alexander*, Gordian II was legate of the governor of Africa, his father, when a revolt erupted in this province against the emperor *Maximinus* in

Sestertius of Gordian II.

238. Associated with his father to the purple cloak, he directed the army of fortune during the battle at the gates of Carthage against the governor of Numidia, Capellianus, who had remained loyal to *Maximinius*. Capellianus commanded the only legion in the region. During the uneven battle, the powerful Legio III Augusta defeated the Gordian army of fortune, and Gordian II was killed in the fray. When *Gordian I* heard the news about the defeat of his troops and the death of his son, he committed suicide. Carthage fell soon after, and a harsh repression befell the whole province. The reign of the first two Gordians lasted only four weeks. However, the uprising in Africa in 238 was only the first in a series of disruptive events characterizing a period of military anarchy, which was to span more than fifty years.

Pupienus *Marcus Clodius Pupienus Maximus*

Place of birth unknown, Italy 164 – Rome, Italy 238
Reign: 238
Senator Pupienus was an intelligent man, well-read and experienced in the military field. He was consul in 205 and then governor in Germania in 210 under *Septimius Severus*. In 225, under the reign of *Severus Alexander*, he was proconsul of Asia before becoming the prefect of Rome. Once the African uprising against the emperor *Maximinus* of 238 was crushed and following the death of *Gordian I*

Silver Antoninianus of Pupienus.

and *Gordian II*, the Senate opposed to *Maximinus* designated two new emperors from its own ranks. Senators Pupienus and *Balbinus* thus donned the purple cloak. Pupienus was unpopular because he had been severe against the people of Rome during his recent urban prefecture. The people, dissatisfied with the choice of the Senate, imposed a third member in the person of *Gordian III*. The latter, then 13 years old, evoked the memory of the first two of the same name to whom he was related. He was designated *Caesar* and successor of the two emperors.

Struggles between the people of Rome, who supported the 'emperors of the Senate', and the Praetorian Guard which remained loyal to *Maximinus* disturbed the capital. While *Balbinus* and *Gordian III* worked to restore order in Rome, Pupienus was responsible for leading the war against *Maximinus*, who was besieging Aquileia. Following *Maximinus*'s assassination by his own troops, the latter submitted to Pupienus, who returned to Rome, victorious.

The disappearance of *Maximinus* and the moderation that characterized the start of the new reign made the future promising, but the Praetorians, opposed to the exercise of power by civilians, would put an end to this illusion of stability. Upon Pupienus's return to Rome, mutual distrust emerged between the two emperors. The Praetorians used the opportunity to assassinate both of them during the celebrations that marked the victory over *Maximinus*. They then proclaimed as emperor the young and more controllable *Gordian III*. The reign of the two emperors lasted only ninety-nine days.

Balbinus *Decimus Caelius Calvinus Balbinus*

Place of birth unknown 178 – Rome, Italy 238
Reign: 238
Very little is known about Balbinus's life and career. According to chroniclers of the time, he was a man characterized by his humanity and his gentleness. He appeared to have been governor of provinces and consul twice, in 211 and 235.

Once the 238 uprising in Africa against emperor *Maximinus* was crushed, Senators *Pupienus* and Balbinus were elevated to the purple

Gold Aureus of Balbinus.

cloak by the Senate that had endorsed the uprising. *Gordian III* was also designated *Caesar* and successor to the two new emperors. In 238, while *Pupienus* was charged with leading the war against *Maximinus*, Balbinus and the young *Gordian III* remained in Rome to preside over the government of the interior and to preserve order. In the capital, unrest had broken out between the people who supported the 'emperors of the Senate' and the Praetorians who remained loyal to *Maximinus*. At the news of *Maximinus*'s death at the foot of the walls of Aquileia and *Pupienus*'s victorious return to Rome, the people and the Senate welcomed the news, but the Praetorians remained unsettled. Still opposed to the fact that the authority was now in the hands of civilians, the Praetorian Guard took advantage of the growing dissension between the two emperors over the primacy of one over the other to assassinate them both. The guard immediately elevated the young and more controllable *Gordian III* to the purple cloak. He was now sole emperor.

Gordian III *Marcus Antonius Gordianus*

Rome, Italy 225 – Zaitha (Al-Salihiyah), Syria 244
Reign: 238–244
During the troubled year of 238, the Senate appointed *Pupienus* and *Balbinus* as co-emperors with the aim of replacing the current emperor *Maximinus*, who had been declared a public enemy by the Senate. When *Maximinus* was killed by his own officers, the two new

Silver Antoninianus of Gordian III.

emperors shared supreme authority. The restlessness of the Praetorians forced the addition of a third member of this particular association in the person of Gordian III. At the age of 13, this grandson of *Gordian I* was named *Caesar* and eventual successor. When the Praetorians murdered both *Pupienus* and *Balbinus* shortly after the death of *Maximinus*, Gordian III was raised to the purple cloak. The Senate and the people approved the appointment by evoking the memory of his grandfather and his uncle, *Gordian I* and *Gordian II* respectively. The legions accepted the nomination of the new young emperor and remained at their posts at the borders of the Empire.

Fortunately surrounded by competent advisors, Gordian III had an imposing task. In 239, the emperor needed to repel the Carpi and the Sarmatians, who had invaded Moesia (central Serbia) and face Sabinianus, the governor of Africa, also proclaimed emperor in Carthage in 240. Once the immediate threats had been neutralized, the 16-year-old emperor married Furia Tranquillina for reasons of succession. By the same token, the father of the bride, Timesitheus, was designated prefect of the court and principal advisor to the emperor. It was a happy event because the intelligence and the loyalty of Timesitheus ensured a favourable reign. Order was restored to the court and the big cities were again supplied with wheat.

In 242, a major military campaign was again required. The Persians, under Sapor I, invaded Roman Mesopotamia and reached the gates of Antioch (ancient city near modern Antakya). Gordian III and Timesitheus left Rome and carried out a victorious campaign by pushing back the Persians behind the borders of the Empire. About to strike a decisive blow in the very heart of Persian territory, Timesitheus succumbed to a violent fever in 243. This disappearance was unfortunate for Gordian III, who quickly became the prey of dishonest officials.

Timesitheus's closest collaborator, the ambitious *Philip the Arab*, thus became courtroom prefect. His thirst for power led him to take advantage of the youth of Gordian III and to declare himself regent of the Empire. *Philip* preferred working to supplant Gordian III and to take the purple cloak for himself rather than to invest his energies against the Persians. Following a few military setbacks blamed on Gordian III, and with the help of shenanigans, *Philip* won the loyalty of the army frustrated by the recent defeats. The circumstances of Gordian III's death have not yet been clearly established. Some authors claim that *Philip* had him secretly murdered. Others suggest that Gordian III was assassinated by soldiers when he tested their loyalty by asking them to choose between him and *Philip*. Nonetheless, when *Philip* announced the death of Gordian III and his intention to succeed him in Rome, the Senate unenthusiastically confirmed him as emperor.

Philip The Arab *Marcus Julius Philippus*

Philippopolis (Shahba) Syria 204 – Verona, Italy 249
Reign: 244–249

Philip appeared on the political scene as military commander under *Gordian III* during the 242 campaign against the Persians. In 243, on the death of the Praetorian prefect Timesitheus, who was the regent of the Empire, given *Gordian III*'s young age, Philip who had been his main collaborator replaced him in this position. An intelligent and ambitious man, he decided to supplant *Gordian III* and take on the purple cloak for himself. With the conviction that he alone could restore the Empire to its former cohesion, he probably had the young emperor assassinated. Before the end of the Persian campaign, he had

Silver Antoninianus of Philip the Arab.

announced the death of *Gordian III* and his elevation as emperor. The Senate confirmed the act with reluctance.

Pressed to get to Rome in order to consolidate his authority, Philip made the mistake of agreeing to a dishonourable peace with the Persians. This act was very badly perceived by the army. On the way to Rome, Philip passed through Moesia and managed to defeat the Carpi and the Quadi but imposed on them a treaty which was not to be respected. The limited war against these Barbarians was Philip's main accomplishment during his reign.

Once in Rome, the emperor organized the celebrations of the millennium of Rome planned for 248. The State's scarcity of financial resources was responsible for the lack of construction activities during his reign. Philip still managed to found a city, Philippopolis (modern Shahba) close to the Syrian hamlet where he was born. It will have been the only Roman city created in the middle of the third century. Philip's reign seemed to have been moderate and characterized by tolerance even on the religious scene. Like *Severus Alexander* before him, Philip was interested in Christianity and did not carry out persecutions. Christianity, until then the cult of the underprivileged, was beginning to infiltrate the aristocracy.

As soon as the millennial festivities ended, disorder erupted and gave way to a serious crisis. In 248, the same legions of the Danube that brought Philip to the purple cloak revolted and proclaimed one of theirs as emperor, Pacatianus. Fortunately for Philip, this Pacatianus was killed by his restless troops a few weeks later. In Cappadocia, another usurper, Jotapianus, was acclaimed emperor. He outlived Philip but was soon assassinated by the same officers who had elected him emperor. In Syria, a certain Uranius also temporarily held the position of emperor before his existence was cut short. During this time, the Barbarians took advantage of these political dissensions to ravage Moesia again.

Philip then decided to give Senator *Decius* the tasks of restoring order in the army and to push the Barbarians out of the Empire. Once the most pressing and difficult mission against Germanic invaders was accomplished, the enthusiastic troops acclaimed *Decius* emperor. The latter decided to head for Rome. Historians are not unanimous on *Decius*'s motives, but Philip who now feared for his position and his life raised an army and charged to fight him. In a battle which took place around Verona in 249, *Decius*'s smaller but exalted army got the upper hand, and Philip was killed during the battle. Thus ended another reign according to the shifting will of the army.

Decius *Quintus Decius Valerinus*

Budalia (Martinci), Serbia 201 – Abrittus (Razgrad), Bulgaria 251
Reign: 249–251

In the middle of the third century CE, the Roman world faced a period of serious difficulties. Barbarian incursions were frequent, and the border regions were devastated. The military, which had become very influential on the political scene, was making and defeating emperors at its whim. The army leaders seemed to be more concerned with their own well-being than that of the Empire they were supposed to protect. The condition of the peasants deteriorated considerably during that time as they remained the victims of frequent passages of armies and of overwhelming taxes. The Senate, whose active role on the political scene had been greatly diminished since the time of the Republic, was now only a representative and barely consultative organization. The balance of the imperial finances had been elusive for some time. A gradual devaluation began to affect the Roman

Silver Antoninianus of Decius.

currency, and inflation was on the rise. During this turbulent period, emperors rapidly succeeded one another. Many had the goodwill and capabilities to reign, but the missing ingredient was time. Not surprisingly, the general context of a permanent crisis and the limited availability of resources made the task of the holder of the purple cloak extremely laborious and perilous. The reign of Decius was a typical example of this.

Originally from the Balkans and married to a woman from a noble and ancient Roman family, Decius was a brave and sensible man. He was consul in 232 under *Severus Alexander* and then became governor of Moesia and lower Germania. From 235 to 238, he was governor of Spain and then prefect of Rome under *Philip the Arab*. During the 248 crisis, *Philip the Arab* instructed Decius to quell armed rebellions in the army and barbaric invasions on the Danube. Once order had been restored in the army and the Goths driven back behind the *limes*, Decius was proclaimed emperor by his victorious and now enthusiastic troops. On his return trip to Italy, a journey whose motives are still debated amongst historians today, *Philip* decided to march against him with an army for battle. The encounter took place near Verona. Decius's troops, smaller in numbers but exalted by the recent victories against Germanic invaders, emerged victorious and *Philip* lost his life in the fighting. As Decius entered Rome, he was confirmed emperor by the Senate.

Characterized by collaboration with the Senate, Decius's reign was short but far from inactive. A conservative and traditionalist man, the emperor was very attached to the State religion. He re-established censorship with the aim of ensuring discipline in the army, ensuring better tax collection and raising the moral standard of all Romans. Censorship, a legacy of the republican period, had been abolished by *Augustus* two and a half centuries earlier. Decius established an annual ceremony during which all citizens of the Empire were to pledge their loyalty to the emperor and to the official religion. The Christians who refused this oath of allegiance were considered traitors to the State and were condemned to die. Thus, a new period of persecution against Christians began. Meanwhile, Decius carried out repair work on the Balkan and eastern routes to ensure maximum mobility for the armies in these regions, which were now constantly under threat of invasion.

Despite the achievements of Decius, the general state of the Empire remained critical. For the positive measures of the reign to bear fruit, a period of stability was necessary. Alas, this luxury was precisely what was lacking. As if the situation were not serious enough, an epidemic emanating from Ethiopia appeared in Egypt and spread quickly throughout the Empire. The plague gripped the Empire for fifteen years. Decius faced serious challenges internally and at the borders of the Empire. In addition to dealing with the usurpations of Priscus and Julius Valens, Decius had to face the Goths who invaded Dacia, Moesia and went as far as to besiege Philippopolis, in Thrace, which was the city of Philip of Macedonia, father of Alexander the Great, not to be confused with the recently founded Philippopolis in Syria by *Philip the Arab*. Once he and his army arrived, Decius was severely beaten. Philippopolis fell and was ransacked by the Goths. While the Goths plundered the city, the emperor regrouped his army and attacked the Barbarians again as they were starting their trek to return to their northern forests, laden with booty and prisoners. The Goths were beaten, but the eldest son and designated successor of Decius was killed in battle.

Decius wished to put an end to the barbarian menace. Relying on arriving reinforcements under General *Trebonianus Gallus*, Decius led another attack against the Goths who were now retreating. The strategy was working, and Decius was about to break the resistance of Goths. At the height of the battle, as planned, *Trebonianus Gallus* was to intervene with his troops for the final blow, but as he secretly wished to replace Decius as emperor, he betrayed him by not attacking as was agreed. With part of his army missing, now fewer in numbers, exhausted, and in a strategically unfavourable position, Decius and his army were massacred, and the Goths regained their forests, laden with loot. This betrayal on the part of *Trebonianus Gallus* caused a Roman military defeat, whose gravity was such that its psychological impact on Roman collective memory was comparable to that of the massacre of the three legions during the Battle of Teutoburg in year 9.

Without *Trebonianus Gallus* realizing it yet, this military defeat and the death of Decius triggered the most unstable socio-political situation that the Roman world had ever known. Military anarchy was at its apex.

Trebonianus Gallus *Caius Vibius Trebonianus Gallus*

Perusia (Perugia), Italy 206 – Interamna (Terni), Italy 253
Reign: 251–253

Senator Trebonianus Gallus was the governor of Moesia when he actively participated in the wars of *Decius* against the Germanic tribes on the Danube in 250. In 251, the Goths forced the *limes* again and the severity of the invasion required the very presence of the emperor. During a decisive battle over the booty-laden Goths, who were attempting to return to their northern forests after looting Philippopolis, the city founded by the father of Alexander the Great, Trebonianus betrayed *Decius* by not intervening in the battle as planned. At the height of the battle, *Decius* was suddenly deprived of part of his army on which he was relying. The advantageous strategic situation became impossible to maintain, and the Roman troops already engaged in the combat were massacred. *Decius* and his eldest son were both killed. Following the carnage, the purple cloak was left vacant, and the remaining members of the Danube army's

Gold Aureus of Trebonianus Gallus.

high command, probably ignorant of the act of betrayal, proclaimed Trebonianus emperor.

Less energetic than his predecessor and in a hurry to return to Rome to be sanctioned for his new task by the Senate, Trebonianus obtained a humiliating peace from the Goths, who returned to their forests with booty and Roman prisoners in tow. Trebonianus's betrayal did not seem to be generally known. Rather, the defeat was perceived as the result of *Decius*'s failed strategy. The purple cloak sanction was therefore done without difficulty. Once in Rome, Trebonianus adopted *Decius*'s second son, Hostilian, in order to further legitimize his authority. Hostilian died the following year, victim of the plague that was crippling the whole Empire. It was then that he associated his own son Volusian to power. Trebonianus drew popular esteem when he took the necessary measures to 'properly dispose of' the victims of the plague, whether they were rich or poor.

Shortly after the new emperor arrived in Rome, the Persians, having just defeated the army of the East, invaded Roman Mesopotamia and then Syria. At the same time, the Balkans were attacked from the North by the Germanic Carpi and the Burgundians. Trebonianus did not intervene and let the ravaged provinces fend for themselves.

Aemilian, who replaced Trebonianus as the governor of Moesia, temporarily repelled the Germanic invaders beyond the Danube and was in turn proclaimed emperor by his own ardent troops. Disenchanted with Trebonianus's inactivity and apparent powerlessness before the enemies of Rome, *Aemilian* decided to go to Rome in order to depose Trebonianus and replace him. Now urged to protect his throne and his life, Trebonianus requested the assistance of General *Valerian*, the commander of the Rhine legions, to fight *Aemilian*. However, *Aemilian* was the first to arrive in Italy. After gathering troops, Trebonianus decided to fight *Aemilian* himself in Terni. Facing the enthusiastic troops of *Aemilian*, Trebonianus's smaller army of fortune refused to wage a suicidal battle for an emperor who had lost all credibility. Trebonianus and his son Volusian were therefore killed by their own troops, who decided to join those of *Aemilian* as he entered Rome in triumph.

Aemilian *Marcus Aemilius Aemilianus*

Girba (Djerba), Tunisia 207 – Spoletium (Spoleto), Italy 253
Reign: 253
In the middle of the third century, the Empire was in crisis and was attacked on almost all fronts. The *limes* of the Danube were more than once breached, and armed Germanic bands crisscrossed the Balkans and spread terror and desolation wherever they went. In 252, a new wave of invaders crossed the Danube. The new governor of Moesia, Aemilian, senator, ex-consul and above all a brilliant general, replaced *Trebonianus*, who was now emperor. He gained popularity with the soldiers because of his success against the Barbarians. In 253,

Silver Antoninianus of Aemilian.

his troops proclaimed him emperor, and all of the East recognized his elevation. Determined to dislodge and replace the seemingly incapable *Trebonianus*, Aemilian headed for Rome. About 50 kilometres north of Rome, in Terni, Aemilian faced the army assembled by *Trebonianus*. The latter requested the assistance of *Valerian*, the commander of the Rhine legions, but these reinforcements were not to arrive in time. Faced with Aemilian's enthusiastic army, the demoralized and makeshift army led by *Trebonianus* refused to wage a suicidal battle for an emperor who had lost all credibility. *Trebonianus* and his son were massacred by their own soldiers.

Aemilian's reign was very brief but seemed to be characterized by moderation and by a positive attitude with the Senate. *Valerian*, who had been summoned by *Trebonianus* to assist him to fight Aemilian, was still on his way to Rome. At the news of *Trebonianus*'s death, *Valerian*'s troops proclaimed him emperor. Faced with *Valerian*'s army, which was more imposing, Aemilian's army decided to decline an armed confrontation. Aemilian was in turn abandoned by his soldiers who joined *Valerian*'s legions. Aemilian was promptly assassinated by those same troops who had brought him the purple cloak three months earlier. He who lives by the sword…

Valerian *Publius Licinius Valerianus*

Place of birth unknown 195 – Bishapur (near Faliyan), Iran 260
Reign: 253–260

Commander of the Danube legions in 253, Valerian was summoned to Rome by the Emperor *Trebonianus* to help him fight *Aemilian* who was marching toward the capital with his army to take the purple cloak. Before Valerian's arrival in Italy, *Trebonianus* was killed in the battle against *Aemilian*, who afterwards was confirmed emperor by the Senate. Three months after *Aemilian* was elevated by his troops, those same soldiers murdered him in Spoleto. The incident took place as *Aemilian*'s army faced the imminent arrival of the larger army of Valerian, also proclaimed emperor by his soldiers after the death of *Trebonianus*.

Gold Aureus of Valerian.

Valerian was an aristocrat from an ancient Roman family, an uncommon quality among emperors since the beginning of the second century. Thanks to his origins and military merits, the ex-consul was warmly welcomed and confirmed emperor by the Senate. In addition, the Senate remembered Valerian's active role as a senator in the Senate's opposition to *Maximinus*'s tyrannical rule.

As soon as he arrived in Rome, Valerian, aged 58, associated his son *Gallienus* to power. In these troubled times, minds began to absorb the idea that the Empire was difficult to govern by only one person. While Valerian governed the East, his son and co-emperor *Gallienus* governed the West. This power-sharing practice, awkwardly initiated by *Caracalla* and *Geta*, the sons of *Septimius Severus*, but established by Valerian, led to the establishment of a Tetrarchy under Emperor *Diocletian* thirty-two years later. Valerian pursued *Decius*'s religious policies which went against Christians. Contemporary Christian chroniclers described this period as that of the second great persecution.

When Valerian was confirmed emperor, the Roman Empire was in a very precarious state. In addition to the destructive struggles between its generals for supreme power, the Roman army seemed to have lost its vocation to defend the Empire and acted more in a mercenary fashion. At the same time, the simultaneous assaults of the Germanic tribes and the Persians on the extended borders of the

Empire made it practically indefensible. Taking advantage of this vulnerability, the enemies of Rome penetrated deep inside the *limes*, leaving destruction and desolation in their path. Despite the repeated military victories of some of the emperors of this half of the third century, their success was only partial.

While *Gallienus* was engaged in containing the Germanic tribes on the other side of the Rhine, Valerian was struggling with the Germanic incursions in Asia Minor and on the Lower Danube and was about to face the most formidable adversaries of Rome: the Persians. By 256, Valerian had to concentrate the bulk of his forces against the Persians, leaving the Balkans and Asia Minor to their own devices. Despite the fact that his army was decimated by the plague, Valerian successfully drove the Persians out of the Empire until the disastrous year of 260. To add to the misfortunes of the time, while Valerian's army was besieged in Edessa, the emperor was treacherously captured while negotiating with the King of the Persians, Sapor I.

Valerian was probably killed by his captives after being humiliated and broken; however, his body was never found. For the first time in Roman history, an emperor was taken prisoner and killed by an external enemy. When the Persians, weighed down by the booty they had just looted in Syria, began to return home, Odaenathus, prince of Palmyra and subject of Rome, attacked and beat them, and then pushed them back to the other side of the Euphrates. Self-confident and knowing that Rome was now unable to maintain its authority in the region, he declared himself King of Palmyra. Following the secession of Gaul, which took place in the same fateful year, another part of the Empire had broken away from the control of Rome. The capture of Valerian triggered a serious crisis. Independent states were formed at the borders of the Empire and were expanding at its expense; moreover, the assaults of the Barbarians on the Rhine and Danube frontiers increased in intensity. *Gallienus*, now sole emperor, ruled over Italy, Africa and the devastated Danubian provinces. The Empire appeared to be on the verge of collapse.

Gallienus *Publius Licinius Egnatius Gallienus*

Place of birth unknown 218 – Mediolanum (Milan), Italy 268 Reign: 253–268

Son of *Valerian*, Gallienus was associated to power with his father when the latter was confirmed emperor by the Senate in 253. According to chroniclers of the time, Gallienus was a literate man who appreciated Hellenic philosophy and culture. In 253, the Roman Empire was in a very precarious state. Internal struggles within the army were frequent and the army no longer seemed to be capable of protecting the borders which were attacked in several places at the same time. Taking advantage of the situation, Germanic invaders and the Persians penetrated deep into the interior of the Empire. Despite repeated military victories against the enemies of Rome, the positive effects of these successes were only limited and temporary.

While *Valerian* was fighting the Persians in the East, Gallienus was assisted by Generals Postumus, *Aurelian* and Ingenuus to carry out a long war of attrition in order to hold back the pressure caused by the arrival of new Germanic populations beyond the Rhine. In 258, it was on the Danube that the barbaric threat became most critical in the West. While Gallienus and *Aurelian* led the fighting there, Postumus and Ingenuus had the task of defending the Rhine. It was during that time that Ingenuus, one of Gallienus's best generals, and another usurper, Regalianus, rose up against him. Gallienus had

Gold Aureus of Gallienus.

to again strip the *limes* of troops to defeat them. The Franks then took the opportunity to cross the Rhine and enter Gaul, push into Spain and even make it as far crossing the Pillars of Hercules (Strait of Gibraltar) to land in Mauritania (modern Morocco), plundering everything in their path. At the same time, the Juthungi and then the Alemanni entered the Rhone Valley and northern Italy before being beaten and repulsed by the Roman army, which was being decimated by the plague and weakened by internal struggles.

Then the fateful year of 260 began. Postumus, charged by Gallienus to defend the Rhine, was proclaimed emperor by his troops. Gallienus was fully absorbed in the defence of Italy against the Germanic assaults that had resumed. Without Gallienus being able to intervene, Postumus organized Gaul, Britannia and Spain into an entity independent of Rome. But the worst was yet to come. When his father and co-emperor *Valerian*, who was fighting in the East and whom Gallienus has not seen since 253, was captured by the Persians in 260, the situation seemed desperate. Gallienus, now reigning alone, had to deal with many contenders, a civil war in Sicily and the secession of the kingdom of Palmyra. Much of the East thus escaped Roman control. In 262, to add to all these tribulations, violent earthquakes shook Rome, Africa and part of Asia Minor. Postumus successfully carried out the defence of the Rhine; and Zenobia, wife and successor of the deceased Odaenathus, carried out the defence of the Euphrates frontier. Gallienus, who did not have the means to fight them to retake control of these territories, concentrated his reduced resources to defend Italy against the multiple assaults of the Germanic invaders. The Decumatian Fields (a territory of strategic defence between the Rhine and the Upper Danube), which had become impossible to defend, were abandoned by Rome.

During the extremely eventful reign of Gallienus, reforms were nevertheless carried out. In 260, after the disappearance of *Valerian*, Gallienus put an end to the persecutions of Christians with an imperial decree. The Christians, whose numbers were increasing, remained relatively at peace until 303. Gallienus experienced stormy relations with the Senate, which he excluded from military commands. This practice, adopted by his successors, led to the final separation of civil and military careers. The titles in both spheres became hereditary. The army retained its predominant role in the Roman world and began to change its appearance. The metallic breastplate and the large rectangular shield, characteristic of heavy Roman infantry, began to disappear to make way for generally lighter armour on motley troops. This was perhaps a result of the impoverishment of the imperial treasury, or more likely the result of an adaptation to the type of combat of the more lightly armed Germanics warriors. As a novelty, Gallienus set up a light mobile unit strategically stationed in Mediolanum (Milan) in order to be able to react more quickly to an invasion. Because of the repetitive invasions of this middle of the third century, cities began to build permanent walls and defences.

The middle and lower classes of Roman society suffered greatly from the economic ruin that resulted from internal turmoil and invasions. The devalued currency barely circulated, and inflation was on the rise. The world of art and culture was also affected by the situation of impoverishment and general insecurity. There were few visible initiatives in this area.

Having remained loyal to the emperor until 268, Gallienus's closest lieutenant, Aureolus, was in turn tempted by the purple cloak when Gallienus was away waging a campaign against Germanic invaders who had launched another important incursion into Roman territory. After being beaten by the emperor, Aureolus and his army took refuge in Mediolanum. The besieged city was on the verge of falling into the hands of Gallienus when he succumbed to an attack planned within his own staff. Before dying, the energetic Gallienus designated one of his generals, *Claudius Gothicus*, as his successor. When Gallienus died in 268, the general state of the Empire was very bad. Despite the commendable efforts and the numerous military campaigns put forth by *Valerian* and Gallienus, there was nothing to predict a return to the prosperity of yesteryear.

Claudius Gothicus *Marcus Aurelius Claudius*

Sirmium (Sremska Mitrovica), Serbia 214 – Sirmium (Sremska Mitrovica), Serbia 270
Reign: 268–270

A man of modest origins, Claudius Gothicus seemed to have a strong character and a just moral sense. His military qualities made him rise quickly during his successful military career. General under *Gallienus* during the campaigns against the Goths, he distinguished himself in combat. At the end of *Gallienus*'s reign, he commanded a cavalry reserve corps and was considered first in the hierarchy after the emperor, therefore his successor. During the siege of Mediolanum (Milan) in 268, *Gallienus*, who was fighting the usurper Aureolus, was assassinated by his own generals following a conspiracy. Before dying, the emperor handed over the purple cloak to Gothicus. Members of the Senate were happy to see their persecutor *Gallienus* disappear, among other things because he had denied them access to military commands and positions as provincial governors. The Senate immediately confirmed Gothicus in his new functions.

When Gothicus became emperor, the Roman world had reached an exceptional level of disorder. Three decades of military anarchy had seriously compromised the borders and the integrity of the Roman Empire. After putting an end to the Aureolus rebellion, the new emperor had to drive back the Germanic Alemanni who had taken

Silvered Bronze Antoninianus of Claudius Gothicus.

advantage of the rebellion to go forth into northern Italy. Once this invasion was repulsed, he had to postpone his plan to restore the unity of the Empire by the subjugation of Gaul and the kingdom of Palmyra to face another much more serious invasion. In reality, this invasion was more like a spontaneous migration. In 269, more than 300,000 Gothic, Scythian, Herulian and Gepid men, women and children flooded the Balkans by sea and by land. After months of difficult campaigns, the Romans were victorious, and the Barbarians were either decimated or repulsed. The survivors were integrated into the army or set up as colonists on the abandoned lands inside the Empire, near the *limes*. It is this series of victories that earned the emperor the surname of 'Gothicus' (conqueror of the Goths). The following year, Gothicus arrived at the Sirmium military camp (Sremska Mitrovica) to prepare a counter-offensive against the Germanic Alemanni, Marcomanni and Vandals, who had again invaded the province of Raetia. It was then that the emperor succumbed to the plague still rampant in the Empire.

The gains made by Gothicus were concealed by new territorial losses in the East. In fact, the kingdom of Palmyra under the aegis of the energetic Queen Zenobia had grown with the addition of Egypt and part of Asia Minor taken from the Roman Empire. Zenobia thus cut off Rome from a large part of its grain supply, the staple food of the great cities of the Empire. The short but vigorous reign of Gothicus allowed him to mitigate the most critical threats. However, like so many before him, he ran out of time to demonstrate the full measure of his abilities.

Aurelian *Lucius Domitius Aurelianus*

Sirmium (Sremska Mitrovica), Serbia 214 – Caenophrurium (Marmaraereglisi), Turkey 275
Reign: 270–275
The son of a peasant from Illyria, Aurelian was a poorly educated, severe and rude career soldier, but he was energetic, strong, honest, and endowed with natural intelligence. In 242, under *Gordian III*, he distinguished himself as a tribune at the head of an auxiliary cohort

Antoninianus of Aurelian.

during the campaign against the Sarmatians. In 253, with *Gallienus*, he stood out during the campaigns against the Germanic invaders. Aurelian, who was to become one of the great emperors of the century, was undoubtedly among the conspirators responsible for the assassination of *Gallienus* in Milan in 268, which led to the elevation of *Gothicus*. The most active of *Gothicus's* lieutenants, he obtained command of the mobile cavalry and again distinguished himself alongside the emperor during the campaign against the Alemanni in northern Italy. In 270, *Gothicus* arrived at Sirmium (Sremska Mitrovica) to prepare a counter-offensive against Germanic invaders that had invaded Moesia. *Gothicus* instructed his brother Quintillus to remain at Aquileia with the mission of defending Italy in the event of an attack. When *Gothicus* died at Sirmium that same year, the purple cloak seemed to be destined to Quintillus, but the Danube legions on which Quintillus relied for support declared Aurelian as emperor. Quintillus committed suicide. Aurelian was immediately confirmed for the prestigious, but dangerous imperial office.

Aurelian's reign halted the decline of the Empire that had been triggered by the death of *Severus Alexander* in 235 and even brought about a progressive restoration of the Roman order in Europe. The five-year reign was divided into three phases. During the first, Aurelian pursued what *Gothicus* had undertaken and repulsed the Germanic invaders on the Upper Danube. Once the region became peaceful again, the second phase of his reign began. It was to restore the unity of the Empire. The relative calm at the borders and the absence of usurpers offered Aurelian the necessary leeway to reign properly. That was not the case during the reigns of his immediate predecessors. In 272, Zenobia, Queen of the independent kingdom of Palmyra, declared the total autonomy of her kingdom by removing the effigy of the emperor on her coins. Unable to tolerate this extreme affront, Aurelian decided to retake the dissident territories. Following two campaigns in the East, Aurelian succeeded in retaking the entire East, and the formerly short-lived metropolis of Palmyra was transformed into a military outpost.

Immediately after, the emperor devoted himself to retaking Gaul, also detached from the yoke of Rome. Here again, the time to act was right. Overwhelmed by Germanic invasions on its territory, Tetricus, the 'emperor' of Gaul, already had his hands full when Aurelian's army faced him for battle. Whether this was the result of a secret agreement between Tetricus and Aurelian or necessary after his defeat in battle, Tetricus surrendered. Aurelian spared Tetricus and even made him a senator and governor of Lucania in southern Italy. He died of natural causes a few years later. In 273, the unity of the Roman Empire was restored, and Aurelian began the last phase of his reign, that of reorganizing the Empire.

The authority of the Senate continued its slow decline in the face of increasing imperial absolutism. Even if relations with the Senate remained tense, Aurelian undertook positive initiatives domestically. Food distribution to the poor in Rome resumed and sometimes even included pork and salt. The State's finances were restored thanks to provincial taxes returning to Roman jurisdiction. And thanks to a monetary reform, confidence in the economy was restored as well. There was a slight increase in the quality of the coinage and its precious metal content. The frequency and violence of recent invasions prompted Aurelian to provide Rome with a new wall, no longer making it an open city. The erection of the Aurelian wall, remarkably preserved to the present day, began in 271 and was to be completed during the reign of *Probus* (276–282). Aurelian introduced the worship of the Sun god, Sol, who became the supreme god to whom the Roman deities were subordinated and in whom were integrated deities of many other pagan cults. For the people of the Empire, this novelty, also nurtured by Aurelian's successors, represented another step toward a religious syncretism, the prelude to monotheism which was the predominant element of Christianity.

In terms of external affairs, an important event marked the reign of Aurelian: the evacuation of Dacia in 275, which had been Roman since its conquest by *Trajan* in 107. The precarious geographical situation of this province which suffered the most from the recent tribulations made it too expensive to defend for the benefits owning the territory provided. The strategic decision to evacuate affected two legions and an army of officials who were brought back to the south bank of the Danube. Many civilians and veterans already established in Dacia decided to remain in this now autonomous territory in which Germanic populations would gradually come to blend.

Aurelia's regenerative reign suddenly ended when he was assassinated while preparing an expedition against the Persians. This assassination was devoid of any political character and seemed rather related to a personal vendetta. When Aurelian died, the Barbarians had been repulsed, the Empire had been reunified, the finances had been restored and the State religion had been reinvigorated.

Tacitus *Marcus Claudius Tacitus*

Interamna (Terni), Italy 200 – Tyana (Kemerhisar), Turkey 276
Reign: 275–276
The death of *Aurelian* on the Danube frontier, devoid of any political character, took the army by surprise. Some historians have suggested that the army, apparently in remorse over the effects of its military license, which had brought about the death of well-liked emperors, relinquished the right of choosing a successor to the Senate. Furthermore, the best generals of the time were located far from the Danube. Nonetheless, the soldiers, for want of imminent and unanimous candidates, turned to the Senate to choose a successor. Initially, the Senate hesitated to accept the responsibility, but because

Silver Antoninianus of Tacitus.

it had now been eight months since *Aurelian's* death, it settled the matter and offered the purple cloak to the aged Senator, Tacitus.

A very rich and cultivated man, the ex-consul was appreciated for his personal virtues, his senatorial skills and his military past. Tacitus's general attitude ran counter to the trend that had existed in the imperial circle since *Septimius Severus*. Tacitus functioned by giving back to the Senate part of its former authority on the political scene and to very temporarily reverse the march toward military absolutism. His reign was characterized by collaboration with the Senate and brought certain new measures. For instance, he gave senators access to the posts of provincial governors and of military commands. He prohibited the alteration of currencies and donated part of his own personal fortune to the State for the purpose of carrying out restoration work. The short duration of his reign of around six months did not allow him to carry out other major projects.

In 276, the Heruli again invaded Asia Minor and pushed as far as into Cilicia (southern Mediterranean coast of modern Turkey). The emperor, accompanied by his half-brother *Florianus*, also Praetorian prefect, moved to Cilicia and defeated the Heruli, who began to fall back to the north. Leaving *Florianus* to finish the task of annihilating the invaders before they reached the security of their forests, Tacitus returned to Rome. He was then assassinated by soldiers fearful of reprisals following the assassination of the governor of Syria,

Maximinus, who had behaved obnoxiously but was a relative of the emperor. With the death of the so-called restorer of the Republic, the Senate witnessed the disappearance of the last opportunity it had to regain its authority on the political scene and well as its prestige, both of which had been progressively degraded since *Septimius Severus*.

Florian *Marcus Annius Florianus*

Place and year of birth unknown – Tarsus, Turkey 276
Reign: 276

We know little about Florianus's life before his appointment as Praetorian prefect in early 276 alongside his half-brother Emperor *Tacitus*. That same year, he accompanied the emperor on a campaign against the Heruli, who had invaded Asia Minor and reached Cilicia (southern Mediterranean coast of modern Turkey). Following a swift Roman victory, *Tacitus* set off for Rome, leaving Florianus to finish off the Heruli before they disappeared into the northern forests. Florianus was on the point of annihilating them when he learned the news of the assassination of *Tacitus*. He declared himself emperor, and the West and the Senate recognized him as such. At the same time, in Egypt and Syria, the army of the East proclaimed one of its own, the competent General *Probus*, as emperor. In order to get rid of this competitor, Florianus abandoned the pursuit of the Heruli

Silvered Bronze Antoninianus of Florian.

and left the area to confront *Probus*'s army. The battle took place in Tarsus. Florianus's larger army included Illyrian contingents, some the most formidable troops in the army. However, two decisive factors played against him. The first was the very hot climate of the Cilician summer to which the legions of the North were not acclimatized and in which the army of the East evolved with ease. The second was *Probus*'s nature as a skilful tactician, which was highly respected by the military.

When Florianus's army arrived in Tarsus, *Probus* immediately pushed it on the defensive and the army quickly became besieged inside the city. Following a few armed skirmishes, the loyalty of Florianus's troops began to fluctuate, and a plot within the emperor's own staff led to his assassination. The besieged troops then opened the gates of the city and joined *Probus*. Florianus was the third emperor assassinated in a year.

Probus *Marcus Aurelius Probus*

Sirmium (Sremska Mitrovica), Serbia 232 – Sirmium (Sremska Mitrovica), Serbia 282
Reign: 276–282
Son of a centurion, Probus was a soldier by profession like his father. As a tribune, he took part in *Gallienus*'s campaigns against Germanic

Silver Antoninianus of Probus.

and Sarmatian invaders. Commander of the Illyrian army, he then took command of the entire eastern army under *Aurelian*. General emeritus, Probus was sensible and much appreciated by the troops. When *Tacitus* died in the spring of 276, his half-brother *Florianus* succeeded him with the support of the Senate and that of the legions of the Danube. At the same time, the eastern army chose its own champion in the person of Probus. The clash between *Florianus* and Probus took place in Tarsus. Shortly after Probus began the siege of the city, *Florianus* was assassinated by his troops, who joined those of Probus. The Senate before this fait accompli confirmed Probus as emperor.

Probus's reign began with military campaigns on the Empire's borders, again threatened by Barbarians who, having taken advantage of the instability caused by *Tacitus*'s death, carried out new incursions. In Gaul, since the death of *Aurelian*, the Franks had resumed their raids. In 277, after a series of decisive expeditions, the Franks were defeated. With the Rhine frontier secured, Probus went to the Danube frontier the following year, where he repelled the Burgundians, the Vandals and the Getae. In 279, the emperor eliminated the army of plunderers who had plagued Asia Minor, left by the emperors of Rome to fend for itself for nearly a quarter of a century. Finally, in 280, he travelled to Egypt to inflict a severe correction on the Nubian Blemmyes who had also been carrying out raids in the south of the province. The king of the kings of Persia, intimidated by this renaissance of Roman power and following a few defeats at the borders, begged for peace. In three years, Probus brought back security to the borders of the Empire.

It was only in 281, after bringing peace to the borders and defeating a good number of usurpers, that Probus sojourned in Rome where he organized grandiose games in honour of the recent victories against the enemies of Rome. He completed the wall around Rome begun by *Aurelian* and put in place positive measures on the domestic political scene. For example, since *Domitian* (81–96), cultivating grapevines had been only permitted in Italy. This ban to protect Italian wine production was abolished by Probus, and the cultivation of grapevines spread rapidly throughout the Empire. As did the commercialization of the divine nectar which ensued, thus restoring renewed material prosperity in provinces ruined by the recent invasions.

The Barbarians who survived Probus's military expeditions were integrated into the Empire. Some were assigned to remedy the shortage of manpower in the fields, while others became candidates for the military career which had been gradually abandoned by Roman citizens. The absorption of Germanic elements by the Roman world was certainly not new, but the practice became common under Probus. This tendency was to continue and to become generalized for successors of Probus during the period of the Dominate (285–476). The establishment of Germanic 'colonists' in the provinces, sometimes concentrated in the same area, was not without problems. There was increasing unrest linked to the difficulties associated with the integration of these new populations. The emperor used this new army manpower to carry out public works, such as draining marshes and restoring roads and bridges. Thus, the legions at the borders provided the cities located there with walls. The practice was not new either, but Probus used it more intensely, even too much according to some of his generals.

In 282, Probus undertook a new military expedition against the Persians with the aim of retaking Armenia and Roman Mesopotamia, gradually abandoned by his predecessors. He travelled to Sirmium (Sremska Mitrovica) on the Danube, where troops were gathering for the upcoming expedition. Probably exasperated by the civil works that the emperor had forced it to carry out, the army was agitated. When a suitor in the person of the Praetorian prefect *Carus* was proclaimed emperor by the legions in Raetia and Noricum, the climate was ripe for an insurrection. The troops at Sirmium revolted and Probus was assassinated.

Leaving the Empire in better shape than it was when he took the purple cloak, Probus was able to prove his worth. The borders of the Empire were more secure, and prosperity had reappeared. Here again, the fluctuating allegiance of the soldiers and the lack of loyalty shown by the generals prematurely put an end to a beneficial reign.

Carus *Marcus Aurelius Carus*

Narbo Martius (Narbonne), France 222 – Ctesiphon (near Baghdad), Irak 283
Reign: 282–283

Little is known about Carus's life before 282, when he was a Praetorian prefect under *Probus*. Of modest origins, he made a career in the army. At the end of 282, during the uprising of troops against *Probus* in Sirmium (Sremska Mitrovica), the legions of Raetia and Noricum proclaimed Carus emperor. Following *Probus*'s assassination and thanks to the army's discontent, Carus was recognized everywhere. The new emperor, not having any esteem for the Senate, did not ask for the ratification of his title. The Senate stood aside and found itself faced with a fait accompli. Carus reinstated *Gallienus*'s edict, which excluded senators from provincial governments and military commands. According to many historians, the reign of Carus corresponded to the decisive exclusion of the Senate from the political scene and to the apotheosis of military totalitarianism.

Carus associated his two sons to power as *Caesars*. *Carinus* was responsible for governing the West, while Carus and his second son *Numerian* continued the Persian campaign undertaken by *Probus* in the East. On the road to Persia, Carus defeated the Quadi, who once again threatened the Danube *limes*. The Persian campaign proceeded without much difficulty, and the major cities fell one by one.

Gold Aureus of Carus.

Shortly after the fall of Ctesiphon (near to Baghdad), in the heart of the Persian Empire, Carus died in his tent in a military camp on the edge of the Tigris River in the spring of 283. Some historians proposed that he was struck by lightning, while others alluded to an assassination. However, he was more likely to have died from a brief and violent illness. Without ever having resided in Rome, Carus died far from home after a short reign of ten months, leaving the Empire in the care of his two sons. Nevertheless, he succeeded in providing further stability to the resurgent Empire.

Numerian *Marcus Aurelius Numerius Numerianus*

Place of birth unknown 253 – Emesa (Homs), Syria 284
Reign: 283–284
When *Carus* became emperor in 282, he associated his two sons to power, *Carinus* and Numerian, as *Caesar*s. Eager to continue *Probus*'s expedition against the Persians, *Carus*, accompanied by Numerian, invaded Persia. Meanwhile, *Carinus* remained in the West to keep the Barbarians out of the western borders of the Empire.

On their way to Persia, *Carus* and Numerian defeated the Quadi, who were threatening the *limes* of the Danube. The Persian campaign progressed well. The Persian Empire, weakened by a serious crisis of succession, was unable to resist the Roman legions. Shortly after

Silver Antoninianus of Numerian.

the fall of Ctesiphon (proximity to Baghdad), Emperor *Carus* died suddenly, presumably as a result of a brief but violent illness. He left the Empire to his two sons.

Numerian, still in Persia, was a man with an affable or even weak temper. Some people thought of him more as a poet than a warrior. Preferring rhetoric to political and military questions, he left his father-in-law and Praetorian prefect, Arrius Aper, in charge of operations and command. Aper then launched a long and structured retreat from Persia. As the army was about to cross into Europe, Numerian was found dead in his portable bed with closed canopy where he had retired because of an eye infection. He was probably killed by the order of the ambitious Aper, who wanted to claim the purple cloak for himself. But before Aper could set his plan in motion, another ambitious general named *Diocletian*, probably also involved in Numerian's murder, was proclaimed emperor by the troops. Aper, who was directly associated to the assassination, was quickly eliminated. By the same bloody means that had characterized imperial successions for half a century, *Diocletian* took on the purple cloak. The struggle between *Diocletian* and *Carinus*, no doubt infuriated by the assassination of his younger brother, was inevitable.

Carinus *Marcus Aurelius Carinus*

Place of birth unknown 250 – Margus (Morava), Serbia 285
Reign: 283–285
While Emperor *Carus* and his younger son *Numerian* were fighting in Persia in 283, *Carus*'s eldest son Carinus was charged with governing and defending the West. In Rome, Carinus's behaviour did not live up to his father's expectations. Carinus's depraved private manners, extravagance, tyrannical and arbitrary attitude and even his dress were reminiscent of the time of the odious *Elagabalus*. Carinus, whose sexual appetite was legendary, surrounded himself with incompetent favourites as advisors and adopted a more hostile attitude toward the Senate than that of his predecessors. Carinus was frequently tempted to confiscate senators' property and assets for distribution to the people of Rome. Blinded by the emperor's frequent and extravagant

Gold Aureus of Carinus.

games, they did not seem to suffer from this singular reign. The army of the West remained faithful probably thanks to the recent in-person victories against the Germanic tribes on the Rhine and the Caledonians in northern Britannia. Carinus's reign was generally perceived by historians as a positive one.

When Carinus's brother and co-emperor *Numerian* died in the East, not long after their father *Carus*'s death, a general named *Diocletian* was proclaimed emperor by the army of the East. The ambitious *Diocletian*, who wished to get rid of his rival, gained a foothold in Europe and marched against Carinus. The latter then left Rome to meet him. Taking advantage of the unrest, a man named Sabinius Julianus also claimed the purple cloak. Carinus easily defeated him in Verona before setting off again toward the East. The face-to-face took place in Margus, where Carinus won the battle but was killed during the fighting. According to the chroniclers of the time, Carinus's assassination was linked to his past and had nothing political or military about it. It was suggested that the assassination was perpetrated by one of his officers whose wife had been seduced and mistreated by the emperor. His victorious army, now without a leader, rallied with *Diocletian*'s troops. By a stroke of luck, *Diocletian* became the sole master of the Empire.

This violent change of reigns resembled most of those that characterized the second half of the third century. What was different this time was the presence of a favourable socio-political climate that had not existed for some fifty years. This allowed *Diocletian* to assert his qualities. He was about to establish a lasting legacy that corresponded to the rebirth of military force and the return of an invigorating economic dynamism for the Roman world. A new era of prosperity was about to begin.

Emperors of the Early Dominate (285–395 CE)
The Tetrarchy

Diocletian *Caius Aurelius Valerius Diocles Diocletianus*

Salonae (Split), Croatia 244 – Salonae (Split), Croatia 311
Reign: 284–305

Silvered Bronze Antoninianus of Diocletian.

Maximian *Aurelius Valerius Maximianus*

Sirmium (Sremska Mitrovica), Serbia 250 – Massilia (Marseille),
France 310
Reign: 286–305 and 306–310

Coin of Maximian.

Constantius Chlorus *Caius Flavius Valerius Constantius*

Illyria 250 – Eboracum (York), England 306
Reign: 305–306

Bronze Follis of Constantius Chlorus.

Galerius *Galerius Valerius Maximianus*

Serdica (Sofia), Bulgaria 260 – Serdica (Sofia), Bulgaria 311
Reign: 305–311

Silver coin of Galerius.

Valerius Severus *Flavius Valerius Severus*

Northern Illyria (Albania) year unknown – Tres Tabernae (site south of Rome), Italy 307
Reign: 306–307

Gold Aureus of Valerius Severus.

Maxentius *Marcus Aurelius Valerius Maxentius*

Syria 283 – Rome, Italy 312
Reign: 306–312

Gold Medallion of 4 Aurei of Maxentius.

Licinius *Caius Valerius Licinianus Licinius*

Felix Romuliana (near Zaječar), Serbia 265 – Thessalonica
(Thessaloniki), Greece 324
Reign: 307–324

Bronze Follis of Licinius.

Maximinus Daia *Galerius Valerius Maximinus Daia*

Felix Romuliana (near Zaječar) Serbia 270 – Tarsus, Turkey 313
Reign: 310–313

Gold Aureus of Maximinus II Daia.

Constantine I *Flavius Valerius Aurelius Constantinus*

Naissus (Nis), Serbia 272 – Nicomedia (Izmit), Turkey 337
Reign: 306–337

Gold Solidus of Constantine I.

Enlisted at a very young age in the army, Diocletian stood out during the reign of *Probus*. This general of modest origins, leader in the formidable army of Illyria, commanded the imperial guard after the death of *Numerian* in 284. After having been proclaimed emperor by the armies of the East, Diocletian arranged for the execution of the supposed murderer of *Numerian*, the Praetorian prefect Arrius Aper. Diocletian, who may have also collaborated in the murder of *Numerian*, now had to fight his rival. Taking the lead of his army, he headed on to challenge the army of *Carinus*, the older brother of *Numerian* and emperor in the West. The battle of Margus, which was turning in *Carinus*'s favour, ended when the latter was killed during the clash. *Carinus*'s army then joined Diocletian's, who by this stroke of luck became the sole master of the Empire. Unlike his predecessors, Diocletian was a man of government as well as a man of the sword. His personality was forged by intelligence and political sense as well as by feats in battle. Diocletian's reign marked the beginning of what modern historians call the Dominate. This period corresponded to the culmination of absolutist tendencies which ultimately prevailed over the traditions of the Principate inaugurated by Emperor *Augustus* three centuries earlier.

Diocletian's reign was innovative in many ways. The most striking was undoubtedly the creation of the Tetrarchy. This system of government where authority was shared between two and then four men began in 286 when Diocletian associated Maximian to power. An uneducated man of modest origins and of brutal morals, Maximian entered the Roman army very early on and distinguished himself under *Aurelian* and *Probus*. He was also a long-time friend of Diocletian. Promoted *Caesar* in 285 by Diocletian, he was elevated and associated to power with the title of *Augustus* the following year. It was the first step toward the Tetrarchy. Like Diocletian, Maximian held the title of *Augustus*, but it was Diocletian who made the final decisions. Given the immensity of the task of governing the Empire, this political concept had been making its way into the collective consciousness for more than a century.

From 286 to 289, while Maximian was waging war in Gaul and on the Rhine against the Barbarians and was ruling the West, Diocletian governed the East. In Gaul, Maximian suppressed an uprising of the Bagaudes, looting bands composed of peasants driven from their lands during the recent invasions. He then carried out a military campaign against the Franks, the Burgundians, the Alemanni and the Heruli, who had taken advantage of the disorder caused by the Bagaudes to venture within the borders of the Empire. In the East, Diocletian carried out military expeditions against the Germanic tribes and the Sarmatians on the Danube before obtaining a new peace treaty from the Persians that gave back to Rome part of Mesopotamia and authority over Armenia.

In 293, the diarchy was transformed into a tetrarchy with the appointment of two deputies with the title of *Caesar*. These tried-and-tested military leaders assisted the two *Augusti*. In addition to facilitating the management of the Empire, this measure was intended to simplify the succession process by avoiding the emergence of usurpers and internal armed conflicts, which were major problems in the middle of the third century. Diocletian was now assisted by Galerius in the East and Maximian by Constantius Chlorus in the West. Galerius was a valiant fighter in the army of Illyria who resembled Maximian with his modest origins and rough morals. He stood out on the Danube border at the beginning of the Diocletian-Maximian diarchy. He was in his thirties when Diocletian adopted him and designated him *Caesar*. Constantius Chlorus was also an excellent soldier despite his fragile health. This educated man served with distinction in the army under *Aurelian* and *Probus*. Having a moderate temperament, he had a disdain for unnecessary violence. Present in Diocletian's entourage for several years, he was in his forties when the *Augustus* of the West Maximian adopted him and designated him *Caesar*.

There was a subtle hierarchy among the members of the Tetrarchy: Diocletian had predominance over Maximian as *Augustus*, and

Statue of the
Tetrarchy in Venice
in 1995 and …

Constantius Chlorus, over Galerius as *Caesar*. Despite this distinction, they all had the imperial prerogative. From 293 to 297, Diocletian and Galerius fought a Germanic incursion on the Danube before passing through Egypt and Palestine and then consolidating the *limes* against Persia. Galerius distinguished himself again on the Danube against Germanic attacks. Then, after a difficult campaign, he succeeded in obtaining a lasting peace agreement from the Persians. Constantius Chlorus reconquered Britannia, which seceded in 286, and Maximian pacified the *limes* of the Rhine. Constantius Chlorus then replaced Maximian on the Rhine, while the latter headed

Statue of the Tetrarchy in Venice in 2010.

off to Africa to inflict severe punishment on the desert tribes, the Kabilian Quinquegentianis (confederation of five Berber populations of Numidia), who were making incursions into Roman territory. Some of Rome's defeated enemies were relocated within the Empire in depopulated border areas.

Internally, as well as externally, there was a revival of the Roman State and society after half a century of turmoil and decline. The supreme power of the four rulers was coupled with a divine cult attributed to them. The Senate was kept apart but tolerated. Its role was now limited to the legal field. The Gregorian and Hermogenian Codes, which recorded the acts decreed since Hadrian, were a new development in law. The final separation of the civil and military professions was completed with the imposition by imperial decree of the hereditary aspect of careers. Recruitment into the army was now mainly carried out among candidates of Germanic origin, colonists from outside the Empire, and sons of soldiers. The army's strength increased from 300,000 to 400,000 men. Administrative reforms were also taking place. Diocletian increased the number of provinces in order to improve their respective management and to reduce the likelihood of provincial insurrections. The provinces now reduced in size were grouped into dioceses.

In addition to undertaking new construction and restoring the Empire's existing infrastructure, a financial reform was undertaken to improve the economic health of the State. The minting of gold and silver coins resumed, and the quality of minting increased. Rome also lost its role as sole imperial residence. The cities of Trier, Milan, Thessaloniki and Nicomedia took over this honour for a time. Here began the decline of Rome's direct role in the affairs of State.

Another important event marked the reign of Diocletian: the last great persecution against Christians. It began in 303 and lasted until his death in 311. The probable causes of Diocletian's resumption of persecutions were undoubtedly related to the uncontrollable parallel authority that the Christian Church represented in the eyes of the authorities. Christians did not recognize the divinization of emperors, and the refusal of many to participate in pagan ceremonies became common. Defenders of the State religion were also concerned about their ever-increasing numbers.

To everyone's surprise in 305, Diocletian and Maximian retired from public life. The former, ill, may have believed his work complete. As for Maximian, possibly displeased, he did so as he had been bound by a promise. The two *Caesars*, Constantius Chlorus and Galerius, in turn became *Augusti*. Before dying peacefully in his palace at Spalato (Split) in 311, Diocletian witnessed the ruin of the Tetrarchy. The dissensions between his successors eventually incited armed struggles for the supreme authority. Despite these setbacks, in the eyes of modern historians, Diocletian's work was very positive, and the Empire was strengthened.

According to the basic principles of the Tetrarchy, the primacy of the *Augusti* was to fall on Constantius Chlorus but Galerius, younger and more vigorous, imposed himself. Maximian's son, Maxentius, and Constantius Chlorus's son, Constantine I, were the ideal candidates as *Caesars*. However, Galerius, gifted with a strong character, preferred to impose two individuals whom he could better control as instruments of his own will. He therefore chose Valerius Severus, a military man and boorish companion of long standing, and Maximinus Daia, a nephew with brutal morals who was also a military man. Even though Constantius Chlorus was *Augustus* in the West, his situation was perceived as precarious because of the appointment of Galerius's comrade, Valerius Severus, as his deputy, and *Caesar*. A rivalry soon developed between the fallen candidates and the designated ones.

In 305, the authority of the Roman world was shared, but not divided, into four regions managed by one of the four emperors. *Augustus* Constantius Chlorus governed Britannia and Gaul, while his deputy *Caesar* Valerius Severus managed Italy, Spain and Africa. In the East, *Augustus* Galerius administered Illyria and Asia Minor, while Egypt and the rest of the East was under the control of *Caesar* Maximinus Daia. In 306, joined by his son Constantine I, Constantius Chlorus was in Britannia to put down a local revolt initiated by the Picts. Already ill, Constantius Chlorus died a year after being appointed *Augustus*.

When Constantius Chlorus died in 306, tensions exploded. Constantine I, who was at his father's death bed, was proclaimed *Augustus* by his troops. Maxentius took advantage of the discontent in Italy regarding the heavy financial burden imposed by Galerius through Severus to start an uprising and proclaimed himself *Augustus* also. Maximian, regretting having left political life, came out of retirement to resume his former title of *Augustus* at the invitation of his former deputy Galerius. The latter, who tried to dispel the confusion, appointed the recently appointed *Caesar*, Valerius Severus, as *Augustus* and a substitute for Constantius Chlorus. In 307, Valerius Severus was killed while fighting Maximian and Maxentius temporarily allied, but the confusion remained. There were now four *Augusti*: Galerius, Maximian, Constantine I and Maxentius, and one *Caesar*, Maximinus Daia.

In November 307, Diocletian presided over an official meeting in Carnuntun with the aim of re-establishing order and the tetrarchy, but Galerius's authority greatly influenced the results. It was decided that Galerius remained *Augustus* and a newcomer, another friend of his, Licinius, was to replace Valerius Severus recently deceased as *Augustus* without having been first appointed *Caesar*. Maximinus Daia remained *Caesar* and Constantine I was demoted to the same rank. The new hierarchy was intended as follows: Galerius and Licinius were recognized as *Augusti* and Maximinus Daia and Constantine I as *Caesars*. In spite of the Carnuntun conventions, disputes persisted, and the document was without effect. Maximian simply refused to recognize the conventions, and the two *Caesars*, annoyed by Licinius's non-conforming elevation, had their troops proclaim them *Augusti*. As for Maxentius, he decided to keep his title of *Augustus* and kept Italy and Africa under his jurisdiction. In 310, the confusion was at its peak. There were six *Augusti*: Galerius, Licinius, Maximian, Maximinus Daia, Constantine I and Maxentius, and no *Caesars*. Maximian, abandoned by Maxentius and pursued by Galerius, took refuge under the protection of his son-in-law Constantine I. Maximian then began to envy his son-in-law's success. Conspiring to overthrow him, Maximian was arrested and executed. Following the natural death of Galerius in 311, four *Augusti* remained: Maximinus

Daia and Licinius in the East, and Maxentius and Constantine I in the West. There were still too many of them for peace to persist. The struggle for supremacy continued in both parts of the Empire.

Showing a sustained respect for Roman traditions, Maxentius demonstrated real competence in the administration of his provinces. He carried out extensive road work and restoration. Even though he was a pagan, he did nothing against the Christians. His main shortcoming was his lack of military experience. This was to cause his downfall. From 310 on, his popularity declined because of the heavy financial burdens he imposed on senators and the aristocracy, as Galerius had done before him. Most of the money raised was used to bribe the soldiers of Valerius Severus and Galerius, who both had wanted to eliminate Maxentius from the political chessboard by invading Italy. In 312, in Rome, the exasperated Senate asked Constantine I to free the city from Maxentius's rule. Constantine I was only waiting for a pretext to get rid of this rival. With the assurance of non-intervention from Licinius, Constantine I descended from Gaul with an army of 40,000 men to face Maxentius, who commanded a larger but disparate and scattered army.

Having secured northern Italy to protect its rear in the event of an attack by Maximinus Daia or a betrayal by Licinius, Constantine I headed straight to Rome. Hitherto entrenched behind *Aurelian's* wall surrounding the city, Maxentius decided to take the initiative by making an exit to fight Constantine I in open ground. As a result of tactical errors, Maxentius and his troops found themselves facing Constantine I's army with their backs to the Tiber River near the makeshift wooden bridge they had just crossed, near the stone Milvius Bridge. In this disadvantageous position, Maxentius's troops yielded at the first engagement. It was a debacle. In order to re-enter the city, Maxentius's soldiers rushed to the bridge, which gave way under the weight. Many drowned and Maxentius was among the victims. Only the Praetorians remained on the battlefield to be killed on the spot while fighting. Maxentius's body was found the next day in the river. His disappearance made Constantine I the sole master of the whole West.

Since the abdication of Diocletian and Maximian in 305, Christians were tolerated in the West, but they remained persecuted in the East by Galerius and Maximinus Daia. In 311, shortly before his death, Galerius issued an edict of tolerance which officially put an end to the persecutions of Christians. But as soon as his death came, they began again under Maximinus Daia, whose aim was to revive the classical Roman religion. He continued the persecutions in Asia and Egypt until his death. In the rest of the Empire, a relative religious tolerance reappeared. In 313, Constantine I openly condemned the persecutions of Maximinus Daia when an alliance was forged between him and Licinius, Maximinus Daia's rival in the East. Not having assisted his ally Maxentius against Constantine I a year earlier, Maximinus Daia, now isolated, was driven to take up arms against Licinius for supremacy in the East. In April, following some limited military success, he fought Licinius's smaller army in Thrace, where he was defeated by his opponent's military genius. Having become a fugitive, Maximinus Daia took refuge in Cilicia to gather new troops. Before he could put his plans in action, Licinius's army caught up with him. Encircled in Tarsus and acknowledging his lost cause, Maximinus Daia committed suicide. With his death, only Constantine I and Licinius remained in the political arena.

At this point, it seemed conceivable that the Empire could be governed by two *Augusti*, but this possibility quickly vanished. Despite the marriage of Licinius to Constantine I's half-sister, the sharing of power became an issue because of Constantine I's ambition since he tolerated his rival only out of obligation. When the schism between the two *Augusti* became apparent in 316, Constantine I was solely responsible for it. The cause of this rift was a disagreement over the choice of *Caesars*. Constantine I, who was just waiting for the pretext to get rid of his last rival, prepared to act accordingly. When he decided to unleash hostilities, he led his army to the Danube, where he defeated Licinius's larger army at the Battle of Cibalae. Licinius, driven back into Thrace, regrouped his forces and fought a second battle near Adrianople, the result of which was inconclusive. Negotiations led to a peace that was to last five years. The agreement considerably increased the size of the territory controlled by Constantine I, with the annexation of the Balkans, but his intentions were now clear to everyone.

During this period, the two emperors ruled over their respective territories, but Constantine I was concerned about the question of his succession. He had three sons: *Constantine II, Constantius II,* and *Constans*. He was again at odds with his associate in the East who named his son Licinianus *Caesar*. Constantine I's intention was to replace both with his own sons. The context favoured him. Constantine I presented himself as the champion of the Christians and his support for them, whose importance and numbers were increasing, had become a significant advantage. Even though Licinius showed religious tolerance in the East, he was not favoured by the Christians. Licinius encouraged pagan philosophy and was sceptical of Christians, whom he tolerated until 320. From then on, his attitude hardened and eventually became persecutory when he began to suspect them of plotting against him in favour of Constantine I. This change of attitude may have been well founded, but it was nevertheless a mistake that was to prove fatal. Licinius was now deprived of significant civilian support, and this situation led to significant desertions in his army when hostilities broke out again. The situation exacerbated the political conflict by giving it a religious character.

In 324, war broke out again. Constantine I and an army of 130,000 men arrived in the outskirts of Adrianople, where Licinius was waiting for him with 165,000 soldiers. Following a decisive battle, Licinius was defeated. He reorganized his forces and locked himself in Byzantium where, at sea, the rival fleets clashed for two days. With his fleet also defeated, Licinius and what was left of his army made their way to the coast of Asia Minor in a vain attempt to regroup and drive back Constantine I's troops who are pursuing him. Once again defeated at the Battle of Chrysopolis, Licinius then took refuge in Nicomedia where he finally capitulated. At the request of Licinius's wife, Constantine I's half-sister, Licinius was kept alive. But Constantine I had him murdered six months later in Thessaloniki, where he had been exiled. At the end of 324, nothing remained of the Tetrarchy set up by Diocletian in 293. Constantine I was now the only master of the entire Empire, whose unity had been restored, and paganism was no longer the official State religion.

From 325 until his death in 337, Constantine I reigned alone. This twelve-year period was far from a peaceful end to his reign. In fact, the most significant events of the reign took place then. In the military field, the concept of the mobile army initiated by *Gallienus* was finally instituted by Constantine I. Part of the frontier troops were grouped into mobile units stationed in strategic locations inside the Empire. The long-term effects of this reorganization for the defence of the Empire are not unanimous among modern historians; but most agree that in the short term it was very useful for Constantine I during the military campaigns that followed against the Barbarians. In fact, in 328, the emperor inflicted a severe defeat on the Alemanni on the Rhine and then carried out a large-scale victorious campaign against the Goths on the Danube. In 334, he massively attacked the Sarmatians and temporarily brought back under Roman control most of Dacia, abandoned by *Aurelian* in 275.

Although proven a great military leader, Constantine I may not have been such a good administrator. But he had the wisdom to surround himself with competent and loyal advisors who managed the Empire on his behalf. Under Constantine I, within the now theocratic State,

Arch of Constantine I in Rome.

imperial protocol was heightened, and the centralization of power was further accentuated. In 330, Byzantium, which the emperor adorned with numerous buildings was renamed Constantinople, or City of Constantine (modern Istanbul). The city became the new Christian capital of the Roman Empire. It thus took on the torch from the thousand-year-old pagan Rome, which ultimately lost its pre-eminence. Even the Praetorian Guard in Rome, an institution founded by *Augustus* more than three centuries before, was dissolved. There was, however, a dark side to the picture. Constantine I's wars and numerous architectural achievements were expensive. In spite of a financial reorganization, the imperial administration raised taxes significantly.

Without openly condemning the pagan religion, Constantine I continuously worked to win the favour of the Christians by building churches and establishing 'moral' laws. The emperor also intervened directly in the affairs of the Church. Perhaps the most obvious example was the convening of the Council of Nicaea in 325. No sooner had Licinius disappeared than Constantine I had to deal with a religious crisis. Since the doctrine of the new religion was not yet officially established, there were different dogmatic Christian interpretations circulating, including Arianism. Confrontations and sometimes destructive passions were unleashed. Constantine I mandated the council, probably more to safeguard public order than out of spiritual conviction. He brought together the various religious authorities of the time to define the dogmatic bases of Christianity and to eliminate interpretations deemed deviant.

In spite of the palace intrigues that led to the execution of his son Crispus, born from a first marriage to Minerva, and then of his second wife Fausta, Constantine I's succession was still assured by his three other sons: *Constantine II*, *Constantius II*, and *Constans*. In 337, while planning to conquer Persia, Constantine I became seriously ill. It was said that it was on his deathbed that he was finally baptized. When the remains of the first Christian emperor were brought back to his new capital, Constantine I left his three sons a strengthened empire.

Constantine II *Flavius Claudius Constantinus*

Arelate (Arles), France 316 – Aquileia, Italy 340
Reign: 337–340

When in 316, the *Augustus* in the East *Licinius* raised his son to the rank of *Caesar*, *Constantine I*, the *Augustus* in the West, did the same with his sons Crispus, from a first marriage to Minerva, and Constantine II, then a very young child, from a second marriage to Fausta. If the protocol of the Tetrarchy still seemed to be followed, it was only in appearance, because contrary to the stipulations of the basic principles, the *Caesars*, this time, were obviously not chosen on merit, but rather by birth. When Crispus and Fausta were executed for treason in 326 by *Constantine I*, who by that time was sole emperor, Constantine II was 10 years old. He was now the oldest of three brothers, *Constantius II*, who was about 9 years old, and *Constans*, who was 6. In 332, during his father's military campaign against the Goths on the Danube, Constantine II, then aged 15, was appointed titular commander of the army fighting the Visigoths. The following year he moved to Trier, where he was given the ceremonial title of protector of the Rhine River *limes*.

When *Constantine I* died in 337, his will established that the Empire was henceforth to be governed by his three sons and two of his nephews, Dalmatius and Hannibalianus. Even today, historians still question the rationality of this decision on the part of *Constantine I*. Whatever the motives behind these provisions, this

Bronze coin of Constantine II.

association of emperors soon proved to be impossible to maintain. By mutual agreement between the three brothers, the two nephews were quickly taken out of the picture. Gaul, Britannia and Spain fell under Constantine II; Italy, Africa and the region of the new capital Constantinople, under *Constans*; and the Orient, under *Constantius II*. Interestingly, although all three sons of *Constantine I* were Christians, they divinized their father after his death, a practice that went against their new faith. This act might have been explained to some extent by the fear of displeasing a large part of the population that still remained pagan.

If the primacy between the three emperors belonged by right to Constantine II, because he had been the first among his brothers to be raised to the title of *Caesar*, he never succeeded in asserting it definitively. After a short period, discord arose. The primary cause of this tense situation was *Constans*'s rejection of the primacy of Constantine II. A meeting took place in Pannonia between the three emperors, where an attempt was made to define the boundaries of each other's domain and to settle the question of predominance. During this meeting, *Constans*'s personality seemed to have guided the decisions. He inherited the Balkans from *Constantius II*, perhaps the one with the weakest character among the three brothers. Of course, this meeting did not settle the question of predominance, and so war seemed inevitable.

In 339, with the assurance of the non-intervention from *Constantius II*, who was fully committed to fighting the Persians, *Constans* openly rejected the predominance of Constantine II. When *Constans* left Italy in 340 to fight a Germanic invasion of the *limes* of the Danube, Constantine II decided to invade the peninsula. During the subsequent military campaign, Constantine II was killed in an ambush organized by the vanguard of *Constans*'s army, which, alerted about the invasion, had arrived from Illyria.

Constans I *Flavius Julius Constans*

Place of birth unknown 323 – Vicus Helena (Elne) France 350
Reign: 337–350

Constans was the third and last son of *Constantine I* and Fausta. Raised at the imperial court of Constantinople, he obtained a solid education and studied Latin. When Crispus, *Constantine I*'s first son from a first marriage to Minerva, and then Fausta were executed for treason in 326, Constans was only 6 years old. In 333, *Constantine I*, wishing to ensure his succession, raised his last son to the rank of *Caesar*. Constans thus joined his two brothers, *Constantine II* and *Constantius II*, in this capacity. In 337, when *Constantine I* died, Constans became *Augustus* like his two brothers and inherited part of the West to govern.

When *Constantine II* died following a short war with Constans over the primacy of the emperors, the whole of the West reverted to Constans, while *Constantius II* ruled the East. An intelligent reign was plausible, but religious differences between the emperors quickly eliminated the prospect. On the one hand, *Constantius II* showed sympathy for the Arians, who represented the predominant Christian doctrinal interpretation in the East. On the other hand, Constans, the only one of the three brothers to have been baptized, distanced himself from the Arian Christians and stood as the defender of Catholic Orthodoxy which remained faithful to the resolutions of the Council

Bronze coin of Constans.

of Nicea of 325. Catholic Orthodoxy was the dominant doctrinal version of Christianity in the West. The divergence between the brothers came to light at the Council of Serdia in 342, where Constans defended Athanasius, the patriarch of Alexandria exiled from the East by the Arian authorities. Civil war was about to break out in 346 when the two emperors forged a reconciliation without enthusiasm. In the West, Constans initiated a persecution against the different Christian doctrinal versions of Catholic Orthodoxy, including the Arians and Donatists, in addition to persecuting pagans and Jews.

On the external affairs scene, Constans carried out victorious military expeditions against the Franks in 341–342, and the following year he went to Britannia where he conducted military operations beyond Hadrian's Wall. Modern historians do not really understand why Constans was not liked by the army and his regime seemed unpopular. It was possible that his attacks against paganism shocked a large part of public opinion and the army. We only know that this dislike was to bring about his downfall. In 350, in a palace conspiracy, Constans was dethroned by the commander of his army named *Magnentius*. Immediately, the troops abandoned Constans in favour of the new *Augustus*. Constans, attempting to flee to Spain, was captured and killed by one of *Magnentius*'s lieutenants.

Constantius II *Flavius Julius Constantius*

Sirmium (Sremska Mitrovica), Bulgaria 317 – Mopsuestia (Yakapinar), Turkey 361
Reign: 337–361

Constantius II was the second son of *Constantine I* and Fausta. After the final defeat of *Licinius* in 324, *Constantine I* became the sole master of the entire Empire. He then granted the title of *Caesar* to Constantius II, who was then 7 years old. The latter thus joined his older brother *Constantine II*, who had already obtained this title. At the death of Constantine I in 337, Sapor II, the King of the Persians, broke the peace treaty that had been signed with *Diocletian* forty years earlier and launched a series of attacks in Roman Mesopotamia with the aim of taking control of the fortresses there. No sooner had

Coin of Constantius II.

Constantius II become *Augustus* in the East that he became heavily preoccupied with war in that part of the Empire.

After the death of his older brother *Constantine II* in 340, the West was again in turmoil ten years later when his younger brother *Constans* was overthrown and then killed under the orders of the general *Magnentius*, who became the *Augustus* in the West. Shortly afterwards, the legions of the Danube also chose an *Augustus* in the person of General Vetrurio. Following a period of indecision, the general renounced and reaffirmed his loyalty to Constantius II, thus reducing the latter's precarious situation who, far from the West, was absorbed by the war against the Persians. Constantius II, who did not recognize *Magnentius*, had the opportunity to act against him in 351. Sapor II had been forced to temporarily cease his attacks on the eastern borders of the Roman Empire in order to defend the eastern borders of his own kingdom against incursions by nomadic tribes. This suspension of hostilities, which lasted until 358, allowed Constantius II to take the initiative against *Magnentius*. At the head of his army, *Magnentius* fought Constantius II at Mursa. Constantius II, who was victorious, continued his campaign by invading Italy the following year. In 353, *Magnentius* was defeated again in Gaul. Shortly afterwards, he committed suicide.

The Empire was reunited under a single emperor, but the cost was high. The colossal destruction of manpower during this campaign, both in numbers and troop quality, did irreparable damage to the Roman army. In the Battle of Mursa alone, considered one of the bloodiest battles of the fourth century, the best legions of the Empire slaughtered each other, leaving 54,000 dead, more than one eighth of the entire Roman army. Constantius II decided to stay in the West for a while to erase the traces of the recent civil war and to repel Germanic invaders who had taken advantage of the disorder to cross the Rhine. The *Augustus* was very much involved in the religious questions of his time. In the arena where passions linked to religious debates were confronted, Constantius II sided with Arianism. This dogmatic interpretation, which in short opposed the concept of the Trinity in the representation of the unique god of Christianity, was widespread in the East. Its founder, Arius, who had been excommunicated at the Council of Nicea in 325, was rehabilitated after his death by Constantius II.

During his stay in the West, Constantius II appointed a cousin, Constantius Gallus, as *Caesar* and charged him with maintaining order in the East during his absence. Acting as a ruthless tyrant, Constantius Gallus was executed before Constantius II had time to meet with him to discuss his behaviour. Realizing that the situation in the East required his presence, he designated Constantius Gallus's half-brother, *Julian*, to the title of *Caesar* and charged him with governing the West. After having spent a few years in Rome, Constantius II returned to the East in 357. On the way, he inflicted defeats on the Sarmatians, the Suevi and the Quadi who were again threatening the Danube frontier. However, he had to hurry back because Sapor II, having settled his problems at the remote eastern borders of his kingdom, had resumed his attacks in Mesopotamia. After almost two years of continuous warfare, the Persians achieved some success by taking some Roman strongholds in the area.

In 360, out of distrust or to respond to a tactical necessity, Constantius II requested *Julian*, who was fighting Germanic incursions on the Rhine, to send reinforcements to the East to assist in the fighting against the Persians. This call for help was perceived by *Julian*'s generals as an attempt by an envious *Augustus* to undermine the position of a very popular *Caesar* among his troops and the citizens of the regions he was governing. These generals refused to leave their posts and bestowed upon *Julian* the title of *Augustus*. The latter accepted the election without apparent resistance. Upon learning the news, Constantius II, as the head of part of his army, once again set off westward in order to remove *Julian*, whom he considered a usurper. Having barely arrived in Cilicia, Constantius II succumbed to a sudden and violent fever.

Constantius II's personality was difficult to explain. While some contemporary authors described him as unwise and impressionable, Constantius II more likely simply had a weaker character than that of his two brothers, *Constantine II* and *Constans*. But the results were clear. He ruled justly and was successful in keeping in check the then most formidable external enemy of the Empire, the Persians.

Magnentius *Flavius Magnus Magnentius*

Ambianum (Amiens), France 303 – Mons Seleucus (La Bâtie-Montsaléon), France 353
Reign: 350–353

Born of a Briton father and a Frankish mother, Magnentius represented a good example of the transformation the Roman army had been experiencing for a century and a half. The entry of Germanic elements into the legion became more pronounced in the third century and was now a predominant phenomenon. It was now common to see soldiers of Germanic origin reaching the upper echelons of the military hierarchy. As a member of a Germanic contingent in the army under *Constantine I*, Magnentius commanded two elite legions under the sons of *Constantine I*. In 350, he was part of a palace conspiracy that overthrew and assassinated *Constans* and became *Augustus* by the acclamation by his troops.

The new emperor had to face a nephew of *Constantine I*, Nepotianus, also declared *Augustus*. After the latter's defeat, Magnentius was recognized throughout the West as the restorer of freedom in reaction to *Constans*'s regime. This was even depicted on coins minted during this period. The undecided legions on the Danube, a region which was part of the East, also named for themselves an emperor named Vetrurio,

Silver 9 Siliquae coin of Magnentius.

who shortly after renounced the title and reaffirmed his loyalty and that of the legions he commanded, to *Constantius II*. At war with the Persians, *Constantius II* incited Germanic tribes on the Rhine to harass Magnentius by attacking Gaul. Being aware of an imminent attack by *Constantius II*, Magnentius gave his brother Magnus Decentius the title of *Caesar*. From 350 onward, embassies were exchanged between the two sides without peace being achieved. The following year, hostilities began when *Constantius II*, at the head of his army, arrived in Pannonia and faced the army raised by Magnentius in Gaul, which included contingents entirely composed of Germanic warriors.

The Roman infantrymen's equipment of the fourth century was not as uniformly and heavily armed as that of the second century as shown on *Trajan*'s column. For example, the slatted cuirass and the wide rectangular shield were no longer used and had given way to lighter and disparate armament. At the first confrontation at the Battle of Mursa, *Constantius II* and his much larger army forced Magnentius to retreat with heavy losses on both sides. The Battle of Mursa alone claimed 54,000 soldiers and was recognized as one of the bloodiest battles of the fourth century. In the summer of 352, unable to prevent *Constantius II* from invading Italy, Magnentius was forced to retreat to Gaul, where he was again defeated. At the same time, he lost control of the Rhine *limes*, which had been temporarily invaded by hostile Germanic forces. Magnentius then took refuge in Lugdunum (Lyon) where, realizing that his cause was lost, he committed suicide.

During his reign, Magnentius, who was a pagan, never harmed the Christians. His aim was to rally the Catholics to join him against the Arians who supported *Constantius II*. The Catholics represented a faction of the Christians who adopted the rules established at the Council of Nicea. Magnentius possessed real military, administrative and diplomatic qualities, but the high rate of taxation he imposed on the upper classes of Roman society, including the literate authorities, eventually made him unpopular, which explained the numerous unfavourable portraits of him that were produced by his contemporaries.

Julian *Flavius Claudius Julianus*

Constantinople (Istanbul), Turkey 331 – Frygium (Samarra), Irak 363 Reign: 361–363

Julian and Constantius Gallus were the sons of Julius Constantius, the half-brother of the emperor *Constantine I*. When the latter died in 337, his son *Constantius II*, the *Augustus* of the East, took Julian and Constantius Gallus under his protection. Julian received an education in literature, grammar and classical rhetoric in Constantinople. In 342, *Constantius II*, who was fighting against the Persians, brought the two teenagers close to him at the fortress

Silver Siliqua of Julian.

of Macellum in Cappadocia (region in Turkey close to the Syrian border), where they continued their education, but this time in a strongly Christian environment. Secretly, Julian kept his interest in the classics. When *Constantius II* became the sole master of the Empire in 350, Julian was sent to Nicomedia (Izmit) where he was so strongly influenced by neo-classics that he converted to paganism. Shortly after the forfeiture and death of his brother who had become *Caesar* in 354, Julian was summoned to the court of Constantinople where he pursued his studies.

The following year, *Constantius II* gave the title of *Caesar* to Julian, who was now 24. Shortly after marrying Helena, *Constantius II*'s sister, Julian was commissioned to go to Gaul to lead military operations against the Germanic tribes on the Rhine and to administer the territory. Julian's merits soon became apparent. From 356 to 359, he inflicted severe defeats on the Franks and the Alemanni, sometimes fighting with inferior forces. He even carried out punitive expeditions into Germanic territory, inflicting further setbacks on them. Julian also demonstrated his qualities as an administrator, which resulted in a significant tax cut. The simplicity of his lifestyle combined with his military successes and sound administration of Gaul made him a popular figure with soldiers and civilians alike.

It seemed that *Caesar* Julian's increasing popularity was worrying *Augustus Constantius II*, who was waging war against the Persians and whose troops were beginning to get overwhelmed. In 360, out of jealousy or tactical necessity in the face of a shaky front, *Constantius II* requested reinforcements from Julian still at war on the Rhine. Regardless of the real motives behind *Constantius II*'s request, this call for help was not well received by Julian's generals. They refused to comply and proclaimed Julian *Augustus*. While leading his army to the West to remove Julian, *Constantius II* died of a violent fever.

Now sole master of the Roman world, Julian arrived in Constantinople in December 361. As soon as he was confirmed as *Augustus* and considering himself the defender of the Roman religion, he issued an edict of religious tolerance for the entire Empire, thus removing Christianity from its position as the State religion. Without resorting to direct confrontations, he used the occasion to take action against the Christians by revoking many of the privileges granted by his predecessors. He in fact used his authority to try to reinvigorate the Roman religion. Julian was a very prolific author, and his works were surpassed in distinction only by those of *Marcus Aurelius*. Julian wrote essays, commentaries, speeches, satires and even chronicles of his campaigns against the Germanic tribes. He established a library in Constantinople which held 20,000 classical works.

Julian was a competent administrator. His actions reflected his simple, no-nonsense lifestyle, and the results were positive. He successfully fought corruption, temporarily cut the normally ever-growing imperial bureaucracy and relieved the crushed economy of the eastern provinces that bore the heavy financial burden of the war against the Persians. Although a literate man, he had to once again demonstrate his qualities as a war leader by facing the Persian peril that had become even more threatening since the departure of *Constantius II* from Roman Mesopotamia the year before. In July 362, Julian arrived at Antioch (ancient city near modern Antakya) from where he organized the preparations for a major campaign.

In March 363, at the head of an army of 65,000 men, Julian set off for the heart of the Persian kingdom. Following a victorious thrust, the bulk of the Roman army was at the gates of Ctesiphon (close to Baghdad). Instead of attacking the city, Julian, who did not believe his forces strong enough to succeed, decided to turn back in order to join up with a reserve army left behind. On route, the Roman army was constantly harassed by the Persians. Provisions began to run out, but the Romans' situation was far from critical. In a skirmish with a Persian heavy cavalry unit, Julian was wounded. The wound became infected and Julian succumbed shortly afterwards. Thus died the last emperor who opposed Christianity.

Jovian *Flavius Claudius Jovianus*

Singidunum (Belgrade), Serbia 331 – Dadastana (near Karahisar), Turkey 364
Reign: 363–364

Son of the commander of an elite corps of officer cadets, Jovian also became a member of this corps under *Constantius II* and *Julian*. In 363, Jovian was himself the commander of this elite unit. In June of that year, upon *Julian*'s death, the purple cloak was offered to the Praetorian prefect Saturninius Secundus Salutius, who declined because of his age and frail health. The troops then proclaimed Jovian as *Augustus*. Jovian was a very tall man and generally seemed to exude a cheerful and even sympathetic character. Having an average education, he nevertheless possessed a practical sense and relied on his advisors to rule. It was also reported that he was a philanderer who appreciated food and wine.

At the news of *Julian*'s death and the appointment of Jovian, Sapor II, the king of the Persians against whom *Julian* was waging war, redoubled the intensity of his attacks against the Roman army still manoeuvring deep into Persian territory. The Roman army was now retreating. Jovian, perhaps in a hurry to return to Roman soil in order to confirm his authority, sued Sapor II for peace, but the price for peace was high. The Romans had to abandon five provinces

Bronze coin of Jovian.

that *Diocletian* had conquered on the other side of the Tigris, including the fortresses of Nisibis (Nusaybin), Castra Maurum (on the River Euphrates) and Singara (Sinjar). The Persians also annexed part of Armenia. This peace, considered dishonourable by most contemporaries, nevertheless allowed the starving Roman army to safely return to Roman territory.

Jovian re-established Christianity as the State religion. He also restored the subsidies that *Constantine I* had given to the churches and that *Julian* had subsequently rescinded. The Christian symbol of the Chi-Rho, traditionally instituted by *Constantine I*, reappeared on the shields and standards of the army. Jovian halted at Antioch (ancient city near modern Antakya) and then in a hurry went to the West, leaving the city in mid-winter. He then halted to Tarsus, where *Julian*'s body was brought before being sent to Constantinople. Jovian then ventured to Tyana (ancient city near Kemerhisar) and then to Dadastana (ancient city near Karahisar), on the border of Bithynia and Galatia, where he was found dead in his bed. Several versions exist to explain his death, but none of them points to an assassination. Some authors put forward the hypothesis that Jovian was poisoned by the emanations emitted by the fresh plaster of his recently renovated room. Others suggest suffocation from the smoke from the brazier in his room, while others assume that he died of indigestion after overeating. Jovian was only 33 years old.

Valentinian I *Flavius Valentinianus*

Cibalae (Vinkovci), Croatia 321 – Brigetio (Szony), Hungary 375
Reign: 364–375

A Christian of modest origins and conditions, Valentinian I spent a good part of his childhood in Africa with his father. Senior officer of the army during the campaign of *Constantius II* against the Persians in 360, he was then commander of a division under *Julian* in 362. Exiled to Egypt by *Julian* because he was a Christian, Valentinian I was later recalled by the new emperor, *Jovian*. The emperor charged him with ensuring the loyalty of the army of Gaul, which had been in turmoil since *Julian*'s death. When *Jovian* died without a designated

Gold Solidus of Valentinian I.

or natural succession in 364, the army he was leading to the West stopped at Nicaea, where the generals debated about succession. They elected Valentinian I, an energetic administrator and an excellent soldier. Despite the fact that he reigned with absolute authority, his very good sense of judgment allowed him to rule intelligently in rather difficult circumstances.

Shortly after his accession to the purple cloak, Valentinian I appointed his brother *Valens* as *Augustus* and co-emperor. Valentinian I was in charge of governing the West, while *Valens* governed the East. The sharing of power between the two parts of the Empire had been a common practice since the end of the third century. By this period, the concept of governance-sharing was more a division of power in which the two parts of the Empire evolved increasingly independently, even though the Roman Empire formally remained an indivisible entity. The tradition that had persisted for centuries that one individual could wholly govern such a vast empire was now a thing of the past.

Although the Persians remained a threat since the less-than-honourable peace *Jovian* brokered with them, the region most vulnerable to an immediate threat from the outside was now the Rhine and Danube *limes*, where the Germanic peril required expeditious military action. In fact, shortly after his elevation as *Augustus*, Valentinian I had to react to a devastating invasion by the Alemanni who crossed the Rhine and took the key fortress of Moguntiacum (Mainz). From his imperial residence in Mediolanum (Milan), rather than Rome, because of its proximity to the threatened area, Valentinian I undertook a series of expeditions against the Alemanni who, after being beaten three times, were finally pushed back.

The year 367 was an eventful one for Valentinian I. Anxious to ensure his succession, he associated his 8-year-old son *Gratian* as *Caesar* of the West. Shortly after this appointment, Valentinian I moved the imperial residence to Lutetia (Paris) and then to Ambiani (Amiens) from where he led military operations in Britannia, which was attacked by the Saxons and the Picts. At the end of the same year, he once again moved the political centre of the West to Augusta Treverorum (Trier), from where he successfully began a new punitive military campaign in Germanic lands. He remained in Barbarian territory for a few years, chasing the Alemanni, seeking alliances and enhancing the defensive apparatus of the Empire by erecting complexes of fortifications on the Rhine. Valentinian I, who fully understood the meaning and implications of the Latin phrase *divide ut imperes* (divide and rule), succeeded in mitigating the seriousness of the threat posed by the Alemanni by allying himself with the Burgundians, their hereditary enemies. Through various treaties and agreements, Valentinian I secured the entry of certain bands of Germanic folks into the Empire. Some filled the ever-growing gaps in the army, while others settled on abandoned land in border regions ravaged by recent Germanic incursions.

It should be noted that for a long time now, the profession of soldier had lost its appeal and was no longer financially interesting for Roman citizens. These factors explain the difficulty in recruiting Roman citizens and the enlisting of Germanic recruits who wished to integrate Roman society. Valentinian I laboured to strengthen the army by improving the soldiers' conditions. Their meagre wages were raised to a tolerable level, as was their status. The emperor made it easier for the soldiers to have access to property and offered them seeds and agricultural equipment so they could take care of their needs in peacetime. Thus, settlements were developing around military camps and some of these would later become the capitals of modern European nations.

Valentinian I also worked intensely to improve the conditions of the plebeians, who were too often exploited by the rich and victims of corrupt officials. Valentinian I's initiatives in favour of the plebeians and the significant tax increases he imposed to finance military campaigns were not well supported by the aristocracy and the big landowners. On the religious scene, Valentinian I did not take sides in the rivalry for predominance between the different dogmatic Christian versions or in the struggle they waged against paganism. Despite being a Christian himself, he adopted a policy of universal tolerance in 371 and simply did not intervene in the tumultuous religious debates of the time.

In 374, Valentinian I returned to battle when the Quadi and Sarmatians attacked the Danube *limes* and penetrated into the province of Retia. The emperor at the head of an army arrived at the camp of Sirmium (Sremska Mitrovica) and undertook the task of repelling the invaders. Toward the end of the following year, during an audience granted to a delegation of Quadi invaders, the latter expressed arrogance toward the emperor. Enraged by this affront, the emperor succumbed to a fit of apoplexy.

Upon the death of Valentinian I in 375, his son *Gratian*, then aged 16, succeeded him as *Augustus* in the West, while his brother *Valens* continued to reign as *Augustus* in the East. Valentinian I also left a second son, from a second marriage, *Valentinian II*, who was 4 years old.

Valens *Flavius Julius Valens*

Cibalae (Vinkovci), Croatia 328 – Adrianople (Edirne), Turkey 378 Reign: 364–378

Younger brother of *Valentinian I*, Valens was a member of the residential guard under *Julian* and *Jovian*. His career seemed to stagnate until the day *Valentinian I* became emperor. Initially entrusted by the latter with the responsibility of the imperial stables as a tribune, he was later elevated to the title of *Augustus* of the East by *Valentinian I*, who was responsible for governing the West. Valens' appointment was not unanimous. In 365, a former senior intelligence officer named Procopius

Gold Solidus of Valens.

proclaimed himself *Augustus* with significant support behind him. The following year, at the Battle of Nacolea in Phrygia, Valens emerged victorious over Procopius who was later put to death.

With his position consolidated, Valens turned his attention to the Visigoths, who had supported Procopius and now threatened to invade the eastern Danubian provinces. From 367 to 369, Valens led punitive military expeditions into Visigoth territory beyond the Danube. From 371 to 377, he waged war in the East against the Persians. Before the campaign began, he had to suppress a conspiracy directed against him by a man named Theodorus in Antioch (ancient city near modern Antakya). The war against the Persians aimed to retake the territories ceded by *Jovian* in 364. Despite some military successes on Persian soil, the gains were minimal when a peace deal was signed in 376.

The policy of religious tolerance practised by *Valentinian I* in the West was not shared by Valens. Himself a committed Arian, Valens persecuted the Catholic Orthodoxy. On the death of *Valentinian I* in 375, Valens declared his primacy between the *Augusti* over his young nephew *Gratian*, *Valentinian I*'s successor and *Augustus* of the West. One monument marked his reign: the great Constantinople aqueduct, whose construction began in 368. Its remnants are still visible in the city that is now called Istanbul.

In 376, an alarming number of Visigoths erupted on the Danube and they overflowed into the northern provinces of the Balkans. The recent arrival of a new invader in Eastern Europe, originating from the steppes of Central Asia, was at the origin of this massive spontaneous migration. In fact, the Huns invaded and destroyed the kingdom of the Ostrogoth, located in present-day Ukraine, causing hundreds of thousands of them to flee to the West. This significant demographic shift disrupted their immediate neighbours, the Visigoths, who had settled in the region of the ancient Roman province of Dacia, present-day Romania, just north of the Danube.

This demographic pressure, combined with the fear of the Huns, caused this massive overflow of Visigoths into Roman territory. Their request for protection within the borders of the Empire was accepted by the imperial authorities on condition that they could be counted on to help defend the region against potential invaders. Once the newcomers settled in Thrace, they were almost immediately exploited by local officials. In 378, united under the command of their leader Fritigern, the Visigoths revolted against Roman authority and began to ravage the region, while other bands of Germanic tribesmen took advantage of the disorder to also cross the Danube.

Following initial military successes by local Roman troops, Valens, arriving from Asia, hastily organized a massive attack against the Visigoths near Adrianople without waiting for military assistance from the Western emperor. *Gratian* had sent Valens an emissary carrying a letter advising him of the arrival of reinforcements. Valens' officers had recommended that he wait for *Gratian*'s army, but Valens engaged in battle anyway, seeking the glory that would follow a decisive victory. Over-confident, Valens combined his forces and attacked the Visigothic army head-on, although intelligence reports alerted that additional Visigothic cavalry was nearby. Before the Romans succeeded in breaking the Visigothic infantry, their flanks were attacked by cavalry.

The result was catastrophic for the Romans. Following a bloody battle, the Roman cavalry was routed, and the infantry, now surrounded, suffered annihilation. Valens was most likely killed in the melee, but his corpse was never found. This battle, in which two thirds of the Roman army of the East was massacred, was described by the chroniclers of the time as a prelude to the end of the world.

The destruction of the western army at Mursa in 358, added to this disaster at Adrianople in 378, effectively announced the beginning of the disintegration of the political and social structure of the ancient Mediterranean world in the face of the migratory pressure of the vigorous Germanic nations.

Gratian *Flavius Gratianus*

Sirmium (Sremska Mitrovica), Serbia 359 – Lugdunum (Lyon), France 383
Reign: 367–383
Gratian was the eldest son of the *Augustus* of the West, *Valentinian I.* In 367, while *Valens* was *Augustus* in the East, *Valentinian I* appointed Gratian, then only 8 years old, to the rank of *Caesar* and co-ruler in the West. At the death of *Valentinian I* in 375, Gratian, then aged 16, was confirmed as *Augustus* of the West. Barely five days later, the Danube troops named the young *Valentinian II*, his half-brother aged 4, *Augustus* and co-emperor of the West. Contrary to what might have been expected, Gratian accepted the nomination and did not seek to harm his half-brother. On the contrary, contemporaries claimed that Gratian sincerely cherished *Valentinian II* and that he took steps to ensure his education. Throughout his reign, Gratian did not do anything to suggest that he was considering doing harm to his half-brother.

Gold 1.5 Scripula of Gratian.

It seems that Gratian was an agreeable, cultured young man. It was reported that in addition to being a good speaker and literary connoisseur, he possessed real military leadership qualities. Remaining the senior *Augustus* in the West because of *Valentinian II*'s young age, Gratian surrounded himself with competent advisors. For a while, the main character of his entourage, a man named Ausonius, was the figure responsible for Gratian's temperate reign. The emperor worked to reconcile the imperial authority and the Senate, which had long been removed from the circle of decision-making, but which remained influential because of the origin and wealth of some of its members. Being Christian, probably Catholic, Gratian was strongly influenced by the Bishop of Milan, Ambrose. The *Augustus* cut State subsidies to pagan cults and was the first emperor to remove the appellation of Pontifex Maximus, chief priest, from his exhaustive imperial title.

After settling disturbances related to illegitimate claims to the purple cloak and following a short stay in Rome, Gratian went to Augusta Treverorum (Trier), which served as a base for operations against the Alemanni. He was at the head of a small army patrolling the *limes* of Upper Danube when he heard the news of the Visigoth rebellion in 378. So, he promised his uncle *Valens* to send troops to assist him in fighting the Germanic invaders. As a result of a strategic error on the part of *Valens*, the battle of Adrianople took place before the arrival of Gratian's troops. It was a catastrophe for the Romans. Even *Valens* was killed. The Visigoths, now without serious opposition, plundered and ravaged the Balkans for nearly four years.

Returning to Sirmium (Sremska Mitrovica) in 379, having become the sole emperor of the whole Empire, Gratian appointed his cousin by marriage *Theodosius I* to the title of *Augustus* of the East as a replacement for *Valens* (and because of *Valentinian II*'s young age) and charged him with dealing with the Visigothic threat. The following year, the two *Augusti* carried out joint military operations, which in 382 lead to the establishment of the Visigoths and Alans in Pannonia. In 383, in Retia where he was making preparations for a forthcoming campaign against the Alemanni, Gratian learned that a general named *Magnus Maximus* had been proclaimed *Augustus* by his troops in Britannia. The latter had already crossed the Channel and landed in Gaul. Swiftly, Gratian at the head of an army arrived in Lutetia (Paris) to fight the usurper. Shortly before the confrontation, his own troops, envious of the privileges Gratian had granted to a troop of Alan mercenaries he had just recruited, abandoned him to join Maximus's army. Gratian had to flee. Surrounded by a small troop of loyal soldiers and trying to reach the Alps, Gratian was assassinated by one of his officers who was pretending to be loyal.

Valentinian II *Flavius Valentinianus*

Augusta Treverorum (Trèves), Germany 371 – Vienna (Vienne), France 392
Reign: 375–392

Upon the death of *Valentinian I* in 375, *Gratian* was *Augustus* of the West, although Valentinian II, his half-brother, nominally ruled Italy, Africa and Illyria as *Augustus* also. When *Valens* was killed at the Battle of Adrianople in 378, Valentinian II, who was only 7 years old, was still too young to play a significant role in the succession. In need of someone capable in the East, *Gratian* then designated *Theodosius I* as *Augustus*. Following the usurpation of *Magnus Maximus* and the death of *Gratian* in 383, *Theodosius I* feared for the life of Valentinian II, but was too absorbed by the affairs of State in the East to interfere in the West. He negotiated an end to hostilities

Bronze coin of Valentinian II.

with *Magnus* in exchange for recognition of the latter's authority as *Augustus* over Gaul, Britannia and Spain. Valentinian II retained his authority over Italy, Africa and Illyria. There were again two *Augusti* in the West, although it was difficult to determine whose primacy was superior.

At Gratian's death, the dispute that persisted between Christianity and paganism intensified in the West. In fact, these were the final jolts of a dying paganism. On the one hand, the defenders of paganism argued that everyone was entitled to his or her own customs and beliefs. It was argued that the policy of tolerance beneficial for the Roman State for so many centuries should not be set aside in the face of a particular cult that was momentarily popular. On the other hand, the Catholic camp could not accept this state of affairs because it implicitly called into question the universality of Christianity. In the end, Valentinian II ruled in favour of the Christians. However, strongly influenced by his mother Justina and the master of soldiers, the Frank Flavius Bauto, both Arians, he issued an edict of tolerance toward the Arians, much to the dismay of the Bishop of Milan, Ambrose, and of *Theodosius I*.

In 387, more confident and sure of his authority, *Magnus* decided to claim the entire West and decided to invade Italy, the basis of the authority of Valentinian II. The latter, then 15 years old, and his mother fled to the East to seek refuge with *Theodosius I*. Once *Magnus* was defeated and overthrown by *Theodosius I* the following year, the latter set aside his differences with Valentinian II on dogmatic matters. *Theodosius I* fully recognized Valentinian II *Augustus* from the West, even though he remained in Italy until 391, and Valentinian II's sphere of influence was restricted to Gaul.

When Bauto died in 388, another Frank replaced him as master of the soldiers of Valentinian II. This idol of the troops, Arbogast, was much more arrogant and authoritarian than his predecessor. Faced with Arbogast's growing authority, Valentinian II, who began to fear him, provided him with a missive forcing him to resign. Arbogast reacted by throwing the document at the emperor's feet. This gesture of insubordination was revealing. Shortly after the incident, in 392, Valentinian II was found dead in his palace in Vienna (Vienne, France). He was 21 years old. Arbogast, undoubtedly the instigator of the murder, raised his own 'puppet' candidate, Eugene, as emperor. Eugene was a former Latin and rhetoric teacher who had become a high-ranking administrative official in the West. Arbogast did this in order to assert his own authority, because in reality, it was he who held the reins of power.

Magnus Maximus *Magnus Clemens Maximus*

Gallaecia (Galicia), Spain 335 – Aquileia, Italy 388
Reign: 383–388

Having served in the army in Britannia in 369, then in Africa in 375 under *Valentinian I*, Magnus was the commander-in-chief of the troops stationed in Britannia in 380. He managed to defend the island against Pict and Scot invaders. The troops of the local garrisons, dissatisfied with *Gratian*'s reign, proclaimed the very popular Magnus *Augustus*. Magnus, who seemed to be a sensible man and very capable of assuming his new role, embraced it. Without waiting for events to unfold, he took the initiative to land on the continent with his army in order to fight *Gratian* heading toward Gaul. *Gratian* arrived in Lutetia (Paris) from where he intended to begin his offensive. Following the desertion of his army, who was envious of the privileges *Gratian* had granted to a group of Alan mercenaries he had just recruited, and ultimately his assassination, Magnus annexed Gaul and Spain to his domain.

Gold Solidus of Magnus Maximus.

After setting up his capital at Augustus Treverorum (Trier), Magnus began negotiations with *Valentinian II*, co-emperor in the West who governed Italy, Africa and Illyria, and *Theodosius I*, Augustus of the East. Faced with a fait accompli, *Valentinian II*, only 12 years old and assisted by his mother and the master of soldiers Bauto, accepted Magnus's coup with disenchantment. *Theodosius I*, absorbed in warfare on his own borders, was forced to do the same. In exchange for this recognition of legitimacy, Magnus ceased hostilities.

A fervent follower of Catholic Orthodoxy, Magnus annoyed both the Arians and the pagans. After having ruled competently over his part of the West for four years, in 387, Magnus, surer of his authority, appointed his son Victor (who was only a child) *Augustus* and co-emperor in the West as he decided to get rid of his rival *Valentinian II* by invading Italy. The latter and his mother took refuge in the East under the protection of *Theodosius I*.

Magnus's victory was short-lived. The following year, *Theodosius I* was on the offensive. While Magnus remained in Aquileia, his general Andragathius advanced at the head of his army in Illyria. This time, the troops facing him, mostly composed of Visigoth federates and Hun mercenaries under the personal orders of *Theodosius I*, did not desert to join Magnus's troops. Magnus's army was defeated at Siscia (Sisak). His brother Marcellinus gathered the troops for another armed confrontation at Poetovio (Ptuj), where this time Magnus's forces were ultimately defeated. Having lost everything, Magnus surrendered to *Theodosius I*, hoping to obtain a pardon. When *Theodosius I* arrived in Aquileia, Magnus and his son Victor were taken prisoner and executed.

Theodosius I *Flavius Theodosius*

Cauca (Coca), Spain 347 – Mediolanum (Milan), Italy 395
Reign: 379–395

Son of a senior officer who was a close collaborator of *Valentinian I*, Theodosius I was a member of the officer corps under his father's orders during the military campaigns in Britannia against the Scots and the Picts in 368, then on the continent against the Alemanni between 370 and 372. In 373, Theodosius I was governor of the province of Upper Moesia (Serbia) and carried out military operations against the Sarmatians. After the execution of his father accused of treason by *Valentinian I* in 375, Theodosius I left political and military life and retired to his estates in Spain.

Following the disappearance of *Valens*, *Augustus* of the East, at the Battle of Adrianople at the hands of the Visigoths in 378, *Gratian*, then *Augustus* of the West, recalled Theodosius I from his retirement and charged him with leading the fight against the Visigoths. Following some successes, *Gratian* declared Theodosius I *Augustus* in the East in 379. Until 382, the two *Augusti* fought jointly against the Visigoths, who had ravaged the Balkans, without, however, succeeding in expelling them entirely from the Empire. A compromise was then reached by granting the Barbarians the status of a federate nation. By a treaty of alliance called *feodus*, the Visigoth nation was officially recognized as an equal and independent ally.

Bronze coin of Theodosius I.

In exchange for a territory that was now theirs and the recognition of their customs, the Visigoths owed military service to the Empire. The addition of large non-Roman contingents that were neither integrated nor 'Romanized' into the army of Theodosius I, and soon into all armies of the Empire, was the only immediate remedy for the serious shortage of recruits in the ranks. For a long time now, the profession of soldier had lost its appeal and was no longer financially interesting for Roman citizens. These factors explained the difficulty in recruiting Roman citizens, a situation that had led to the enlistment of large groups of Germanic elements in the army. It was now common to witness the addition of entire and independent Germanic detachments to the army and a significant increase in the use of mercenaries.

To pay for this Germanized army and the use of mercenaries, Theodosius I significantly increased taxes and expanded the imperial bureaucratic apparatus in order to control the rising inflow of money. In the medium and long term, the effects of these measures were not as expected. In fact, more money was coming into the State coffers, but once all this bureaucracy was remunerated, there was little money left. What was perhaps even more serious was the accentuated general impoverishment of the population of the Empire.

Theodosius I was a competent emperor, but it was not his achievements as a political leader that earned him the epithet 'the Great'. In fact, he earned it from contemporary Catholic chroniclers because of his devotion and decisive action in favour of Catholic Orthodoxy. Theodosius I was known for his laws and decrees against all beliefs other than Catholic Orthodoxy. He deployed considerable efforts against paganism, Arianism and even Judaism. His reign also illustrated the growing influence of the Church on the affairs of State. For example, the bishop of Milan, Ambrose, who had a definite influence on the emperor, refused him communion because he had ordered the massacre of a group of citizens in Thessalonica in retaliation for the murder of a senior officer of his army who had behaved shamefully. Only after displaying public repentance did Theodosius I receive communion from Ambrose. This authority of the Church will prove significant for the future; we need only consider the omnipresence of the Church at all levels of society in medieval Europe.

In 394, at the head of his army whose ranks had swelled thanks to a considerable number of Germanic troops and mercenaries, Theodosius I arrived in the West, planning to overthrow a usurper named *Eugene*. At the Battle of Frigidus, the western army led by *Eugene* was annihilated, but at a high cost to the eastern army. By its intensity and significant loss of men, the Battle of Frigidus could be compared to those of Adrianople in 378 and Mursa in 358. One of the deadliest battles of the fourth century, Frigidus caused such heavy losses that the army of the West would never recover. Following the battle, *Eugene* and his generalissimo Arbogast were executed, and the Roman Empire was reunified into a single political entity. But the situation was short-lived because five months later, in January 395, Theodosius I died in Milan, leaving the Empire divided between his two sons *Arcadius* and *Honorius*. Both born of a first marriage to a Spaniard named Aelia Flavia Flaccilla, they had been designated *Augusti* by their father in 383 and 393 respectively. On his second marriage to one of *Valentinian II*'s sisters named Galla, Theodosius I had a daughter who was also to mark history. Aelia Galla Placidia was to become the wife of the Visigoth leader Ataulf in 414 and then the mother of the future *Augustus* of the West *Constantius III* in 417. She was also to give birth to the future western emperor *Valentinian III* in 419.

Divided Empire: Western Emperors (395–476 CE)

Honorius *Flavius Honorius*

Constantinople (Istanbul), Turkey 384 – Ravenna, Italy 423
Reign: 395–423

Honorius was the second son of *Theodosius I* and Aelia Flaccilla. At about the age of 9, in 393, his father raised him to the status of *Augustus* in Constantinople (Istanbul). On the death of *Theodosius I* in 395, he became emperor of the West at the same time as his older brother, *Arcadius*, became emperor of the East. In 395, Honorius was about 11 years old, so managing the affairs of the state fell on the shoulders of his master of soldiers Stilicho. Half Vandal and half Roman, Stilicho was a capable and energetic man. This would prove to be useful as the West was about to go through the most difficult period in its history. Because it was a labour-rich basin, Stilicho wished to annex to the West the Prefecture of Illyria, currently part of the East. By doing so, he triggered a situation of

Gold Solidus of Honorius.

conflict with his eastern counterparts. First secretly, then openly, both sides of the Empire began to harm each other. This could not have happened at a worst time in the Roman Empire's history.

A dominant player in this internal struggle was Alaric, the king of the Visigoths, who was to take advantage of the situation for himself and his clan. Shortly after the death of *Theodosius I*, the federated Visigoths, who had lived on the border of Lower Danube since 382, revolted under Alaric's leadership and ravaged Macedonia and Greece. Athens was sacked. As Alaric was approaching Italy, Stilicho intervened and defeated him in 397, but the latter managed to elude capture. In 401, *Arcadius*, or rather his influential wife, incited Alaric, now master of the soldiers of the Balkans, to invade Italy in the name of the emperor of the East. Alaric was again defeated by Stilicho at Pollenza in 402 and once again at Verona the following year, but still managed to escape. The West had a brief respite from the Visigoths for a few years, but this threat was replaced by even more serious ones. As a sign of the times, Honorius decided to move the imperial residence of Mediolanum (Milan), which he no longer considered safe, to Ravenna, which was more easily defendable thanks to its encirclement by swamps and its access to the sea. Ravenna was to remain the capital of the Western Empire until its disappearance in 476.

In 405, the storm was unleashed over the West when the Ostrogoths, pushed out of the Hungarian plain by the Huns, crossed the *limes* in Pannonia and advanced as far as Italy before being pushed back by Stilicho at the Battle of Faesulae. The following year, Stilicho's preparations for the invasion of the Prefecture of Illyria were again interrupted by a wave of large-scale invasions that swept across the West. Vandals, Swabians, Alemanni, Alans and Burgundians crossed the frozen Rhine. Moguntiacum (Mainz) and Treverorum (Trier) were the first fortified border towns to fall. The invaders crossed the provinces of Gaul without serious opposition, destroying everything in their path.

Primarily absorbed in planning his attack on the East, Stilicho did nothing to stop the progress of the invaders. Faced with this inaction of the western imperial government, a general named Constantine took control of Britannia, part of Gaul and Spain in 407, which he retained until 411. Other usurpations followed. In the meantime, Alaric became increasingly bold and demanded compensation for his non-intervention in the West. Stilicho agreed. In 408, the Roman aristocracy and the Senate, exasperated by Stilicho, declared him a public enemy. His troops revolted, and Stilicho was arrested and executed.

Stilicho was an able leader, but two factors in his foreign policy caused his downfall: his obsession with annexing the Prefecture of Illyria and his apparent complacency toward his fellow Germanic 'kinsmen'. Stilicho's demise precipitated a decline in the West, which was now deprived of its best generalissimo. At the time of his death, a generalized anti-Germanic sentiment swept through the capital and the army. There was not to be another commander-in-chief of Germanic origin in the West for another half-century. The Germanic troops who had served under Stilicho and who now faced growing intolerance joined Alaric's army. With his most formidable adversary gone and deprived of his allowances, Alaric headed to Rome with his reinforced army. Honorius and his chief advisor Olympius succeeded in preventing an attack on the city by conceding a large sum of money.

After repeating a similar scenario the following year, when he even installed and deposed a puppet emperor in Rome, Alaric attacked Rome in 410 after failed negotiations with Honorius. The Eternal City, which had not been captured by an outside enemy for nearly eight centuries, was taken and looted. The shock on the collective conscience of the Roman world was unprecedented. Many chroniclers of the time alluded to the beginning of the end of the civilized world. After three days of looting, Alaric left Rome, taking with him a prisoner, Aelia Galla Placidia, Honorius's half-sister. He then went to southern Italy. While planning the invasion of Africa, Alaric died in Consentia (Cosenza).

For the next decade, *Constantius III* was the predominant military leader of Honorius and then co-emperor in the West. One by one he defeated usurpers in Gaul. In 414, Alaric's successor, Ataulf as king of the Visigoths, married Galla Placidia, who was in her early twenties, without Honorius's consent. During a military campaign,

Constantius III repulsed Ataulf and his Visigoths to Spain, where Ataulf was later assassinated. His successor, Wallia, returned Galla Placidia to Ravenna, the official capital of the Western Empire, and in return the Visigoths were again granted the status of Federates in Aquitaine, Gaul, with Tolosa (Toulouse) as its capital. In 421, Galla Placidia's new husband and co-emperor *Constantius III* died. Having become a widow again, Galla Placidia entered into conflict with the emperor and was driven out of Ravenna in 423. She and her two children, including *Valentinian III*, took refuge in Constantinople (Istanbul). Shortly afterwards, emperor Honorius succumbed to dropsy.

During the reign of Honorius, St Augustine and St Jerome stood out for their dogmatic achievements, which would become the doctrinal bases of Christianity until then without strictly established rites. At the same time, this period corresponded to a decisive phase in the persecution of paganism. We refer, of course, to Stilicho's destruction of the Sibylline books, the most sacred texts of the ancient Roman religion. Like that of his brother *Arcadius*, Honorius's reign was more characterized by the careers of those who led his government than by his own. Some chroniclers raised doubts about Honorius's behaviour, but many argued that he was not an intelligent man. Although Honorius's impact on the affairs of State was negligible, fatal wounds were inflicted on the Western Empire during his eventful reign, namely the sacking of Rome, and the further disintegration of the western army as a result of the numerous military campaigns that took place during his reign.

Constantius III

Naissus (Nis), Serbia year unknown – Ravenna, Italy 421
Reign: 421
This Roman-born general made his appearance on the political scene following Alaric's sacking of Rome in 410. From 411 to 421 Constantius III was the master of soldiers in the West and steered the government under Honorius. His main task was to fight the many usurpers in the West. He began by defeating a general named Constantine in Gaul and then another named Magnus in Spain.

Gold Solidus of Constantius III.

He then succeeded in subduing a man named Heraclianus in Africa. In 413, unable to drive the Burgundians beyond the Rhine, he granted them the status of Federates. The following year, he repulsed the Visigoths to Spain, who, under the leadership of Alaric's successor, Ataulf, was still keeping Galla Placidia, Honorius's half-sister, prisoner. Following the assassination of Ataulf, his successor Wallia agreed to hand Placidia over to the Romans and in return, Constantius III conceded Aquitaine to the Visigoths and gave them the status of Federates once again. Placidia married Constantius III in 417.

Relative peace returned to the West, but a part of Gaul and Spain still escaped imperial authority. In February 421, practically master of the West, Constantius III was elevated to the rank of *Augustus* and co-emperor with *Honorius*. His wife Placidia, who gave him two children, including *Valentinian III*, was also elevated to the rank of *Augusta*.

Perhaps with the intention of reuniting the Empire into a single political unit when *Honorius* died, the *Augustus* of the East, *Theodosius II* refused to recognize the elevation of Constantius III and Placidia. Outraged, Constantius III made a promise to extort this recognition from the East by force. This eliminated any possibility of cooperation between the two political entities, the only possibility of salvation for the West, which was gradually losing control of its own territory. In the meantime, Constantius III's health deteriorated rapidly, and he died in September 421, barely seven months after his ascension. *Honorius* was to remain sole emperor in the West until his death in 423.

Johannes *Johannes*

Place and year of birth unknown – Aquileia, Italy 425
Reign: 423–425

A civil servant, probably of Germanic origin, Johannes rose to the rank of senior imperial notary. He entered the political arena upon the death of *Constantius III*, co-emperor of the West with *Honorius*, in 421. Now a widow, Galla Placidia came into conflict with her half-brother and emperor *Honorius*. In 423, thanks to the efforts of Castinus, master of *Honorius*'s soldiers, Placidia and her two children, including the future emperor *Valentinian III*, were banished from Ravenna, the capital of the Western Empire. Placidia sought refuge in Constantinople (modern Istanbul).

When *Honorius* died shortly afterwards, Castinus wanted at all costs to prevent Placidia's return to Ravenna and the likelihood of *Valentinian III* being proclaimed *Augustus* of the West. Consequently, he invested Johannes with the purple cloak in 423. Johannes knew that his ascension lacked legitimacy and immediately attempted to obtain recognition from his eastern counterpart. He had bronze and gold

Gold Solidus of Johannes.

coins minted with his own bust and that of *Theodosius II*. Johannes sent emissaries to Constantinople, but they were dismissed and sent back. New figures who would soon play an important role on the political and military scene appeared at this time. On one side, there was the young General Aetius who accepted Johannes's elevation and became the director of the imperial residence. On the other, a commander of the African army named Bonifatius who controlled the traffic of wheat that fed the West. The latter was to offer Placidia important financial assistance to overthrow Johannes.

When it became clear to Johannes that *Theodosius II*, who had not recognized him as emperor of the West, was preparing to send an army to the West in order to depose him in favour of the young *Valentinian III*, he sent Aetius to the Huns to request military assistance. The army from the East arriving by sea was led by one of *Theodosius II*'s most competent generals, Ardaburius, assisted by his son Aspar. The campaign began badly for the forces of the East, as a storm dispersed the fleet in the Adriatic. Ardaburius's ship ran aground near Ravenna, the capital of the Western Empire, and his crew was taken prisoner, while the rest of the fleet managed to reach and take Aquileia. Instead of taking advantage of the situation and attacking Aquileia, Johannes preferred to wait for the arrival of Hunnic reinforcements. In the meantime, Aspar decided to attack Ravenna and, after being guided by a shepherd through the swamps surrounding the city, he entered the city without fighting. Johannes was arrested and sent to Aquileia. Johannes, whose short reign was characterized by moderation, was executed in June 425 after being mutilated and humiliated in public.

Valentinian III *Flavius Placidius*

Ravenna, Italy 419 – Rome, Italy 455
Reign: 425–455

Valentinian III was the son of *Constantius III* and Aelia Galla Placidia, *Honorius*'s half-sister. Initially designated by *Honorius* as his heir, he and his sister were exiled from Ravenna, the capital of the Western Empire, with their mother when she fell into disgrace

Gold Tremissis of Valentinian III.

with *Honorius* after the death of *Constantius III* in 421. They then sought refuge in Constantinople (Istanbul) to the *Augustus* of the East, *Theodosius II*. When *Johannes* was raised to the purple cloak in the West after the death of *Honorius* in September 423, *Theodosius II* refused to recognize him and instead supported Placidia's claim for the elevation of the young *Valentinian III*. After the apprehension and execution of *Johannes* at Aquileia in the summer of 425, Placidia and her children entered Rome.

Valentinian III was officially recognized as *Augustus*, but because he was only 6 years old, the government of the West was led by Placidia and the generals. When Aetius arrived from Central Europe with an army of Huns, he learned that the one he was to defend, Emperor *Johannes*, had already been deposed and eliminated by the protégés of *Theodosius II*. Placidia distrusted Aetius, but she was in a delicate situation. She offered him the position of master of the cavalry in Gaul and gave large subsidies to the Huns to persuade them to return home. Aetius, driven from Rome by Placidia, fought with relative success against the federated Suevi and Visigoths, who were trying to expand their territory at the expense of imperial land. Moreover, he repressed the looting excursions of the Franks in Belgium in 427 and 428.

The relationship between Placidia and Aetius remained lukewarm, but Aetius's rising fame lifted him to the supreme position of master of soldiers. Bonifatius, the commander of the African army who had supported Placidia against *Johannes* in the past, arrived in Italy. With Placidia's complicity, Bonifatius decided to get rid of Aetius, whom they considered a threat to Valentinian III. They probably did so wrongly, as there was no indication that Aetius ever had the intention to overthrow Valentinian III. In 432, during a confrontation between the armies of the two generals, Bonifatius was mortally wounded. Following his death, Aetius became the undisputed military master of the West, although power officially remained in the hands of Placidia and the young emperor, who was 13 years old.

After crossing the Rhine in 406 and having passed Gaul to settle in Spain, the Vandals had a new king in 428: Genseric. At the head of his people, he left Spain in order to carve out a kingdom on more fertile land. The Vandals crossed the columns of Hercules (Gibraltar) and landed in North Africa, which they gradually conquered. In 431, Aetius unsuccessfully carried out a military expedition to Africa in an attempt to stop their advance and subject them to imperial authority. Now in a position of authority, Genseric extracted from Ravenna the status of Federate for himself and his people. In 439, the second largest city in the West, Carthage, fell to the Vandals. Genseric declared himself king of an independent kingdom. In 441, Aetius tried again to submit the Vandals to the authority of Ravenna but failed. Africa escaped the control of the Western Empire, which suddenly found itself deprived of its main source of grain and the important revenues generated from the taxes collected from these provinces.

Unable to call Genseric to order in North Africa, Aetius was successful in Gaul, however. With the help of Hunnic mercenaries and Roman troops evacuated from Britannia, which was abandoned, Aetius managed to repel Germanic invaders beyond the Danube between 437 and 444 and severely defeated the Burgundian Federates, who again had tried to expand their domain in Gaul.

The already considerable difficulties associated with recruiting troops for the Roman army became acute following the loss of Britannia and North Africa. These lands were now either property of federated Germanic 'allies' or illegally occupied by Germanic tribes. The loss of income was so great that it had even become difficult to pay the mercenaries. The army, thus weakened and tried by repeated military campaigns, had no possibility of regenerating itself. As a result, it was no longer in a position to decisively subjugate invaders established on the soil of the Empire or to adequately defend its borders.

In 434, when Attila became king of the Huns, they had already carved out a large kingdom in Central Europe, just beyond the Danube. In 450, the new emperor of the East, *Marcian*, stopped paying the subsidies used to buy peace to the Huns. Attila then turned to the Western Empire, which he knew was more militarily vulnerable than the Eastern Empire, to plunder and amass booty. Attila claimed Valentinian III's sister, Justa Grata Honoria, in marriage. He also claimed half of what remained of the Western Empire as a dowry. This ultimatum was obviously rejected. That same year, Placidia died of natural causes.

At the head of the Huns, Attila crossed the Upper Danube in 451 and entered Gaul, where Aetius was waiting for him with a cosmopolitan army of Visigoths, Alans, Franks and Romans. Despite the death in battle of Theodoric I, king of the Visigoths (not to be confused with the future king of the Ostrogoths, 493–526, of the same name, who will also mark history), the Battle of the Catalaunian Fields was a decisive victory for Aetius. It was the only military setback Attila would suffer. In spite of this victory, the Huns remained formidable and trekked to the north of Italy, where they took Mediolanum (Milan) before Attila's sudden death in 453. With the disappearance of the 'scourge of God', his empire was soon torn apart by the various rival groups fighting for succession.

After the victory of 451, Aetius was at the height of his glory, but he had powerful enemies. The Praetorium prefect *Petronius Maximus* and Valentinian III's chamberlain, Heraclius, persuaded the emperor to eliminate Aetius, whom they saw as a threat to their own authority. Aetius was assassinated in 454, and so died the last leader who could have delayed, at least for a time, the disintegration of the Western Empire. *Petronius Maximus's* scheming did not stop there. Bitterly disappointed not to have been appointed master of soldiers by the emperor, a position held by Aetius, he elaborated a second plot, this time aimed at Valentinian III himself. In March 455, through the intermediary of two former Hun officers of Aetius who sought to avenge the death of their commander, *Petronius Maximus* prompted the assassination of Valentinian III. With his death, so ended the Valentinian dynasty in the West, as did the relatively fragile stability that still persisted there.

A significant social event also marked the reign of Valentinian III. Living in Rome despite the fact that the capital of the Western Empire was Ravenna, he devoted himself to the religious affairs of the State. In fact, this was the only aspect of his responsibilities as emperor in which he took a real interest. In 444, he put into effect an imperial decree that recognized the supremacy of the bishop of Rome over the other bishops of the Empire. This was the birth of the papal concept and the establishment of the foundations of the Catholic hierarchy with which we are still familiar today.

Petronius Maximus *Flavius Petronius Maximus*

Place of birth unknown 396 – Rome, Italy 455
Reign: 455

Notary tribune around 415, Petronius was minister of imperial finance around 418. A very wealthy man, he was Praetorian prefect in Italy and then prefect of Rome as consul. Using his personal fortune, he financed the construction of buildings in the Roman forum. Petronius entered

Gold Solidus of Petronus Maximus.

the high political sphere in an infamous way, as he was the instigator of the murder of Aetius and then of the emperor *Valentinian III*. When the latter died in 455, opinions were divided over his succession. *Valentinian III* had no sons and there was no predominant general capable or popular enough in the West to assume the role of *Augustus*. An influential group supported a certain Maximianus, a former collaborator of Aetius. Another group, which included the *Augustus* of the East, *Marcian*, and Licinia Eudoxia, the widow of *Valentinian III*, supported a man called *Majorian*, who was later to be emperor, but in 455 it was Petronius who inherited the purple cloak.

Almost as soon as he became emperor, Petronius married Licinia Eudoxia by force. She refused to collaborate with him because she knew that he was responsible for her husband's murder. Unable to tolerate the affront, she sought the assistance of the king of the Vandals and master of Africa, Genseric, and promised the hand of her own daughter, Eudocia, whom Petronius had just married to his son Palladius, to Genseric's son. As in the past, this request for outside intervention from a barbarian leader in Roman affairs was to be more dramatic, not to say disastrous, for the West than anticipated. When it became clear that Genseric, who was plundering Italy's coastal cities with his powerful fleet, was heading for Rome, Petronius who was preoccupied with organizing his escape, took no action to organize the defence of the city. Losing all credibility, he was abandoned by the Senate, his relatives and even his bodyguards. While leaving Rome, Petronius was assaulted by the populace and massacred. A few days later, the city fell into the hands of the Vandals, who systematically ransacked it. Genseric took with him Licinia Eudoxia and her two daughters, including Eudocia who, once back in Africa, married his son Huneric.

It was difficult to assess Petronius's reign, which lasted just over two months. His career was prosperous, but everything seemed to have changed once he fell into disgrace with Aetius around 453. Chroniclers of the time reported that Petronius was indeed hated by his entourage. We do not really know the reasons for this hatred, but his responsibility for the murders of Aetius and *Valentinian III* may have given us a clue as to why he was so unpopular and what, ultimately, caused his death.

Avitus *Marcus Maecilius Flavius Eparchius*

Augusta Nemetum (Clermont-Ferrand), France 385 – Brivas (Brioude), France 457
Reign: 455–456

Avitus came from a rich and distinguished Gallo-Roman family from Auvergne. Having studied law, he had a very respectable career as an imperial civil servant. A man of many talents, he was master of soldiers and then Praetorian prefect in Gaul in 437. It was in this position that he negotiated peace with Theodoric I, king of the Visigoths, on behalf of Aetius. When Attila at the head of the Huns attacked Gaul in 451, Avitus came out of retirement to convince Theodoric I, with whom he had become friends, to join Aetius's cause against the Huns. This alliance was to be a major factor in Aetius's victory over the Huns at the Battle of the Catalaunian Fields even if Theodoric I died in battle. Theodoric II succeeded his father as king of the Visigoths, and a new relationship of esteem quickly developed between him and Avitus, who may have been his guardian during his youth.

Once again retired in his estates in Auvergne, Avitus was asked in 455 by Emperor *Petronius Maximus* to join his staff. Before Avitus had a chance to respond, he learned of *Petronius*'s death. Theodoric II convinced Avitus to take the purple cloak with the support of the Visigoths. After some hesitation, Avitus accepted the charge when he was acclaimed as *Augustus* of the West by the regular and federated

Gold Tremissis of Avitus.

troops stationed near his home. With the consent of *Marcian*, the Augustus of the East, Avitus crossed the Alps heading for Rome, thereby entering the perilous arena of supreme power.

Avitus's most recent elevation was not unanimously welcomed in Rome, where the senatorial class took a dim view of the elevation of a Gallo-Roman provincial to the purple cloak. Avitus had no time to deal with this barely concealed disavowal, as more serious threats required immediate action. Bands of Germanic tribes, including the Ostrogoths, made incursions from their domain in Pannonia, and the Suevi once again began to expand their territory in Spain at the expense of Visigothic and Roman lands. Even though Genseric had left Rome, the Vandal fleet continued to attack and plunder the Italian coastal cities and to threaten Sicily and Sardinia. In order to assist him in his tasks, Avitus raised as master of soldiers a half-Suevi half-Visigothic who had risen to the highest ranks of the army, Ricimer. Avitus, at the head of an army, headed to Pannonia to repel the Ostrogoths. Meanwhile, Theodoric II inflicted a severe beating on the Suevi in Spain, and Ricimer defeated the Vandal fleet off the coast of Corsica after preventing the Vandals from landing in Sicily.

Avitus's victorious military campaigns could have helped him consolidate his authority on the throne, but complications undermined the positive effect of his successes. Since Africa had been taken away from the orbit of the Empire, the supply of grain to the great cities of the West had become sporadic, and the urban population was particularly vulnerable to frequent food shortages. During Avitus's military campaigns, a famine in Rome fuelled discontent with the regime. To reduce the number of mouths to feed, Avitus discharged part of his army, namely federated troops, whom he still had to pay. There was not enough money in the State coffers, so Avitus had to melt down some of Rome's bronze statues to achieve his goal, an act of desperation that was to fuel the indignation of the senatorial class. It is necessary to remember that the inflow of money in taxes had been greatly reduced since the loss of territories such as Africa, Britannia and the provinces allocated as territory to the Federates. In addition, the provinces of the Upper Rhine and Upper Danube, prey to looters and victims of repeated Germanic invasions, were no longer able to contribute to the state's coffers.

In 456, everything fell apart for Avitus. Ricimer, who was to henceforth make and defeat emperors in the West until 472, took advantage of the widespread discontent in Rome to attempt to depose Avitus. A battle took place at Placentia (Piacenza), where Avitus's smaller army was defeated by Ricimer. Feeling his life threatened despite the promise of safe conduct after being stripped of his authority, Avitus tried to return to Auvergne, but died on the way there. The reign of Avitus was another unfortunate example of an able and well-meaning emperor who failed to achieve any lasting progress due to an unfavourable general situation. In this case, the waste of human valour and genius was caused not only by material causes, but again by the ambition of an unscrupulous rival.

Majorian *Julius Valerius Maiorianus*

Place of birth unknown 420 – Dertona (Tortona), Italy 461
Reign: 457–461

A former military officer, Majorian was recalled from retirement to become commander of the imperial cadet corps by Emperor *Valentinian III* after the assassination of Aetius. When *Valentinian III* was in turn assassinated in 455, Majorian became a candidate for the purple cloak with the support of the *Augustus* of the East, in addition to

Gold Solidus of Majorian.

that of Licinia Eudoxia, *Valentinian III*'s widow. But it was *Petronius*, and then *Avitus*, who were to successively occupy this office. When Ricimer, staff master of soldiers, caused the overthrow of *Avitus* in 456, Majorian was master of soldiers in Gaul engaged in a military campaign against the Marcomanni. Six months passed before a successor was designated emperor. In the West, the power then rested in the hands of Ricimer even if, officially, Emperor *Marcian* was the master of both parts of the Empire. After *Marcian*'s death in 457, his successor *Leo I*, with Ricimer's recommendation, appointed Majorian as *Augustus* of the West.

Still in Gaul, Majorian's first task was to bring order back to the notables of these provinces dissatisfied with the fate of *Avitus*, who was a fellow compatriot. He had to do the same with Theodoric II, king of the Visigoths, who had been *Avitus*'s most faithful lieutenant. Once his position was consolidated, Majorian turned his attention to Genseric and his Vandals, who represented the most serious threat to the West. The emperor managed to repel a Vandal landing in Campania and then regained northern Italy to gather an army with additional contingents of Goths, Huns and Scythians.

In 460, while Ricimer remained in Italy, Majorian and his army and a fleet of 300 ships set sail for Carthago Nova (Cartagena), which was occupied by the Vandals. Following some initial military successes, the Roman fleet was attacked by surprise and destroyed by the Vandals. The expedition was a failure, and Majorian had to ratify an unfavourable treaty in which the Western Empire had to officially and ultimately renounce to retaking Africa. Now deprived of his fleet, Majorian set off for Italy, where Ricimer was waiting for him, plotting to replace him. It was therefore not by chance that a mutiny broke out among Majorian's troops as soon as he reached Italy after crossing the Alps. He was forced to abdicate. Five days later, Majorian was dead, most likely assassinated.

During his reign, Majorian carried out important legal measures, the texts of which were annexed to the code of *Theodosius II* or Theodosian Code. As a general rule, these laws demonstrated a significant effort by the central government to limit administrative and fiscal abuses at the expense of the population. For example, the function of agent who ensured that the grievances of the plebeians were addressed, a position established by *Valentinian I* and subsequently abolished, was reinstated. Some arrears of provincial landlords in financial difficulty due to successive invasions were annulled. In reaction to the initiatives of *Avitus*, who had bronze statues melted down in Rome to pay the salaries of his federated soldiers, a law was established to preserve and protect public buildings and monuments from this kind of fate. Majorian demonstrated a sense of social justice and a willingness to eliminate the Vandal threat. Unfortunately, his inability to do so brought his life to an end.

Libius Severus *Libius Severus*

Lucania (Basilicata region), Italy year of birth unknown – Rome, Italy 465
Reign: 461–465
Three months after Emperor *Majorian*'s death, staff master of soldiers Ricimer appointed a successor. His choice of emperor, who was now only the legitimate representative of his own government, fell on Libius Severus in 461. The authority of this man, whose origins and career were not known, never extended beyond Italy and he failed to obtain the recognition of the *Augustus* of the East, *Leo I*. From the outset, opposition to this puppet regime of Ricimer was evident. The master of soldiers of Gaul, Aegidius, one of *Majorian*'s lieutenants, was the first to show his opposition. A good strategist

Gold Solidus of Libius Severus.

and pious Christian, Aegidius commanded a considerable army but was prevented from descending on Italy because of hostilities with the Visigoths in Gaul. Since the death of Emperor *Avitus* in 456, the Visigoths had renounced their allegiance to Ravenna, the capital of the Western Empire. Aegidius died in 464 before he could put forward his designs against Libius Severus.

Another opponent was the pagan Marcellinus, a brave and educated man. He was the military commander in Sicily and led a large army composed mainly of Huns. His role was to defend the island against attacks from the Vandals. In the face of Marcellinus's opposition, Ricimer tried to bribe his soldiers. Before this ruse was carried out, Marcellinus and his army left the island and headed to Dalmatia, part of the Eastern Empire, where he swore allegiance to Emperor *Leo I*, who gave him the title of master of soldiers of Dalmatia.

In the meantime, the territorial expansion of the Vandals continued with the conquest of Corsica and Sardinia. Their plundering expeditions even reached as far as Egypt. The threat posed by the Vandals was such that even *Leo I* had to deal with Genseric. The emperor was in turn forced to recognize Africa, west of Egypt, as a Vandal possession. Genseric tried to legitimize this conquest by declaring it as a dowry of the Western Empire for the marriage between his son Huneric and Eudocia, the eldest daughter of Augustus *Valentinian III*. In order to strengthen his ties with the imperial family of the East, Genseric proposed the marriage of Placidia the younger, second daughter of *Valentinian III*, to a nobleman from Constantinople named *Olybrius*. Opposed to the advent of Libius Severus as emperor in the West, Genseric also proposed *Olybrius* as emperor. *Leo I* agreed.

Following a military campaign against the Alans, Ricimer returned to Italy to find that his regime was in peril because of powerful opponents. Probably embarrassed, he had to ask *Leo I* for assistance. The latter succeeded in persuading Marcellinus to stop his attacks, but Genseric, who had become defiant, refused to compromise and launched a campaign of plunder on Sicily, which was left to fend for itself, and even on Italy. Then, Libius Severus was found dead, possibly poisoned. It was more than likely that Ricimer had decided to eliminate him in exchange of *Leo I*'s assistance.

Anthemius *Procopius*

Constantinople (Istanbul), Turkey 420 – Rome, Italy 472
Reign: 467–472

Anthemius originated from a family that had long been present in the imperial entourage in the East. His grandfather of the same name had been Praetorian prefect under *Arcadius* and then regent of young *Theodosius II*. His father had been master of soldiers in the Balkans. Following in their footsteps, Anthemius was commander in 453 and then master of soldiers in Thrace from 454 to 467. This highly-cultured general was considered for the succession of *Marcian* as Augustus of the East, but it was *Leo I* who inherited that role in 457. Anthemius accepted the appointment with dignity and remained loyal to the new emperor. Relations between the two men remained strong and sincere thereafter. During the following decade, Anthemius carried out a victorious military campaign against the Ostrogoths in Illyria between 459 and 464, and a second successful one against the Huns who had ventured into the Lower Moesia, now Bulgaria, in 466–467.

On the death of the *Augustus* of the West, *Libius Severus*, in 465, Genseric, king of the Vandals, aimed to have his own candidate, *Olybrius*, raised to the purple cloak. However, *Leo I* who was trying to limit the influence of the Vandals in imperial politics, rejected this candidacy and reigned nominally over both parts of the Empire until 467. That year, the Vandals' raids on the Peloponnese persuaded *Leo I*

Gold Solidus of Anthemius.

to appoint an *Augustus* in the West so as to better coordinate efforts in the fight against the Barbarians. His choice then fell on one of his most faithful collaborators, Anthemius. The omens were favourable, because in addition to the support of the people of Rome, the Senate and the Germanic federated chiefs, Anthemius was assured the support of the staff master of soldiers Ricimer, ratified by the marriage of the latter with his own daughter. Moreover, there was a real desire for cooperation between the emperors of the East and the West. Such a political climate had not frequently manifested itself since the division of the Empire in 395.

As soon as he arrived in Italy, Anthemius, in association with *Leo I*, organized a large-scale military expedition against the Vandals. The Vandal naval bases in Sardinia were attacked and an expeditionary force landed in Tripolitania, in present-day Libya. Despite these initial successes, the campaign turned to disaster. One of the two fleets was destroyed at the hands of the Vandals because of the incompetence of its naval commander. The leader of the second, Marcellinus, was assassinated, most probably at the instigation of Ricimer, who wanted him dead, since he had rallied to the *Augustus* of the East against his regime headed by *Libius Severus* in 465. Anthemius was not at the end of his difficulties. Shortly afterwards he had to face a rebellion of the Visigoths. Under the aegis of their new king Euric, who murdered his brother Theodoric II, the Visigoths attempted again to expand their kingdom in Gaul.

When a Roman army under the command of Anthemius's son was defeated by the Visigoths, Ricimer began to seriously doubt the usefulness of Anthemius. Following the failure of a second combined military expedition to the East against the Vandals in 470, relations between the two men became hostile. Ricimer, who controlled northern Italy, decided in 472 to march on Rome. He thus wanted to depose Anthemius and replace him with *Olybrius*, who had arrived from Constantinople initially to try, in the name of *Leo I*, to reconcile the two men. With the support of the people and the Senate of Rome, in addition to an army of loyal Visigoths, Anthemius organized the defence of the city. *Leo I*, absorbed by internal unrest and border attacks, was in no position to help his ally. Contemporaries also reported that the coffers of the State were emptied by the expeditions against the Vandals. After a three-month siege, the city, where famine was rife, fell to Ricimer, who plundered it. Anthemius, who with the support of the majority of the Roman elite had the merit of governing well, was captured and summarily beheaded.

Olybrius *Anicius*

Rome, Italy 420 – Rome, Italy 472
Reign: 472

Olybrius originated from an illustrious Italian family present in the imperial entourage since *Valentinian I*. In Constantinople around 464, Olybrius married Placidia, the younger daughter of Augustus *Valentinian III*, who was assassinated in 455. Placidia had been brought by Genseric to Africa following the sacking of Rome by the Vandals in 455. After the death of Western Emperor *Libius Severus* in 465, Genseric laboured to have his candidate, Olybrius, elevated to this position. However, the emperor of the East, *Leo I*, who did what he could to limit the influence of the Vandals in imperial politics, rejected this nomination and reigned nominally over both parts of the Empire until 467. That year, the Vandals' raids on the Peloponnese persuaded *Leo I* to appoint *Anthemius* emperor in the West in order to better coordinate efforts in the fight against the Vandals and other Germanic invaders. Five years later, staff master of soldiers Ricimer

C. W. Becker Silver Siliqua reproduction of Olybrius.

decided to get rid of *Anthemius*, who had failed to eliminate the Vandal threat, and attacked Rome. *Leo I* sent Olybrius to Italy on his behalf, with the aim of reconciling the two antagonists. Once he had arrived in Rome, which was already under siege by Ricimer's troops in 472, the latter proclaimed Olybrius emperor of the West. Nothing suggests that Olybrius tried to refute this prestigious but perilous nomination.

Three months later, Rome fell and *Anthemius* was executed. Olybrius then became, in theory, the master of the West despite the fact that the real power resided in the hands of Ricimer and that the territory remaining under imperial control was, in practice, limited to Italy. After dominating the political scene in the West since 455, Ricimer died of natural causes in May 472 and was replaced as staff master of soldiers by his nephew, a Burgundian named Gondobad. The new association did not last. Olybrius, who had not yet had time to influence the course of history, died a few months later.

Glycerius *Flavius*

Place and year of birth unknown – Place and year of death unknown
Reign: 473–474

After the death of *Olybrius* in 472, the Augustus of the East, *Leo I*, was unable to find a capable successor for the West. For the next four months, he was again theoretically the sole master of both spheres of

Gold Tremissis of Glycerius.

the Roman Empire. At the beginning of 473, Gondobad, the master of soldiers of Italy and son of the king of Burgundy, decided to take matters into his own hands and provide the West with an emperor who was in fact the representative of his own government. He chose the commander of the elite corps of officer cadets, Glycerius.

We know nothing of Glycerius's career or life before his elevation. His short reign was dominated by the Ostrogoths' imminent threat to Italy. Following the collapse of the Empire of the Huns around 454, the Ostrogoths regrouped and initiated incursions into the Danube borders of the Eastern Empire. The emperor of the East *Marcian* was forced to allow them to settle in Pannonia with the status of Federates. From 473, under the aegis of a new leader and future king named Theodoric I, not to be confused with the king of the Visigoths of the same name (418–451) killed at the Battle of the Catalaunian Fields while fighting against Attila, the Ostrogoths again became a threat to both parts of the Empire. The Ostrogothic kingdom was enlarged at the expense of Roman territories, and Theodoric I began to set his sights on Italy, the imperial province and last Roman stronghold of the Western Empire. Glycerius was abandoned by Gondobad, who left Italy with his troops to succeed his father as king of the Burgundians. With diplomacy, Glycerius managed to avoid an invasion and was able to divert the Ostrogoths to Gaul.

In the meantime, *Leo I*, not having recognized Glycerius's elevation, sent the master of the Dalmatian soldiers, *Julius Nepos*, to Italy with the aim of overthrowing and replacing Glycerius. Dalmatia was part of the Eastern Empire although by this period, it was a semi-autonomous region. Once *Julius Nepos* arrived in Italy, Glycerius, whose army was significantly reduced since the departure of Gondobad, surrendered and abdicated without bloodshed. Glycerius's life was spared and he became bishop of Salonae (Salone) in Dalmatia. He may afterwards have become the bishop of Mediolanum (Milan), from where, rumours say, he would have orchestrated the assassination of *Julius Nepos* in 480 after the latter had also been deposed as emperor five years earlier.

Julius Nepos *Flavius Julius*

Place of birth unknown 430 – Salonae (Split), Croatia 480
Reign: 474–475

Son of Nepotianus, who was master of soldiers under *Avitus* (455–456), Julius Nepos was also the son of the sister of Marcellinus, master of soldiers of Dalmatia. This territory was nominally part of the Eastern Empire even if in reality it was a semi-autonomous prefecture. When Marcellinus was assassinated at the probable instigation of Ricimer in 468, Julius Nepos assumed the military command of this region. In 474, *Leo I*, not recognizing *Glycerius's* elevation to emperor of the West, offered military support to Julius Nepos to depose him and become the *Augustus* of the West. When Julius Nepos landed in Italy, *Glycerius*, lacking sufficient resources to oppose him, abdicated without bloodshed against the promise to have his life saved.

Almost as soon as Julius Nepos was confirmed in his new functions by the Senate, the Visigoths, under their new king Euric, once again renounced their status as federated and this time declared themselves independent from the imperial authority as the Vandals had done a generation earlier. Unable to counter the advance of the Visigoths, whose possessions were expanding in Gaul, Julius Nepos asked in vain for the assistance of the Burgundian Federates, who preferred not to interfere. Following the fall of Auvergne in 475, Julius Nepos was forced to recognize the independence of the enlarged kingdom of

Gold Tremissis of Julius Nepos.

the Visigoths. From then on, with the exception of a part in the north-west, which remained Roman territory until 486 (i.e., the provinces managed by the governor Aegidius, then by his son Syagrius), Gaul escaped Roman control. Before becoming governor, Aegidius had been the master of soldiers under *Majorian*. At that time, Germanic Gaul was divided between the Franks, the Burgundians and the Visigoths; Spain was divided between the Suevi and the Visigoths; North Africa was part of the Vandals kingdom; and Britannia was being conquered by the Angles, the Jutes and the Saxons.

Faced with the manifestation of apparent powerlessness by Julius Nepos, the master of soldiers of the general staff, a Roman named Orestes, decided to depose the emperor and replaced him with his own son *Romulus*. At the head of an army, Orestes left Rome for Ravenna, the capital of the Western Empire, where Julius Nepos resided. The latter did not believe Ravenna safe and knew that he could not count on the assistance of the new emperor of the East, *Zeno*, who himself was temporarily expelled from the capital by his political opponents. Consequently, before the arrival of Orestes, Julius Nepos left the city and found refuge in Salonae (Split).

The following year, after the defeat and death of Orestes, *Romulus* was also forced to abdicate by the new Germanic master of soldiers of the general staff, Odoacer, who was proclaimed king of Italy by his soldiers. Before the end of the year 476, the emperor of the East *Zeno* received two delegations from the West successively: the first, from Odoacer, asking the emperor to ratify the fait accompli in Italy in exchange for the recognition of the supremacy of *Augustus* of the East; the second, from Julius Nepos, requesting the support of *Zeno* and military assistance in order to restore his position as *Augustus* of the West. Unable to intervene in the affairs of the West, *Zeno* was forced to recognize Odoacer as king of Italy but summoned him and the Senate to recognize Julius Nepos as *Augustus*. Gold coins were minted in the West on which the effigy of Julius Nepos as emperor appeared, but Odoacer did nothing more. Julius Nepos was assassinated in 480 in Salonae (Split) without ever seeing Italy again.

If history reports that the political existence of the Western Roman Empire officially ended in 476, when *Romulus* was deposed by

Odoacer, it is significant to point out that this date is in fact only an academic landmark that may seem artificial. Let us recall that although the political existence of the Western Empire had already been precarious for a generation, Julius Nepos lived until 480, and we know nothing about Emperor *Glycerius* after 474 or about Emperor *Romulus* after 476. Furthermore, the last Roman-held lands, the kingdom of Soissons under the leadership of governor Syagrius, resisted invasion until 486.

Romulus Augustus *Flavius Romulus*

Place of birth unknown 460 – Neapolis (Naples), Italy, year of death unknown
Reign: 475–476
Romulus was the son of Orestes, a high-ranking civil and military official of Roman origin who worked at the court of Attila. When Attila died in 453, Orestes enlisted in the army of the West. His military qualities and experience made him progress rapidly through the ranks. In 475, he was appointed master of soldiers of the general staff by *Julius Nepos* and obtained the status of patrician, that is, member of the Roman aristocracy. Thanks to his experience with the Huns and his contacts with the Germanic kings, Orestes secured the support of the senior officers of Germanic origin, who made up almost the entire officer corps of the western army.

Gold Solidus of Romulus Augustus.

The senior officers of what remained of the army of the West were dissatisfied with the elevation of *Julius Nepos* as emperor, as he had been imposed by the emperor of the East. Following the loss in Gaul of the region of Auvergne to the Visigoths, the popularity of *Julius Nepos* was at its lowest. Outraged by this apparent incapacity, Orestes took the initiative to try to depose him and set off for Ravenna, the capital of the Western Empire, at the head of an army. After the departure of *Julius Nepos* from Ravenna, Orestes refused to be elevated as emperor as desired by his generals. Instead, he named his son Romulus to the charge, then aged 14. The emperor of the East, *Zeno*, who recognized *Julius Nepos* as emperor of the West, declared the elevation of Romulus as illegitimate.

For the previous fifty years, because of successive invasions and massive migrations, the Roman emperors of the West had been forced to recognize with reluctance the formation of Germanic kingdoms within the Empire itself. Loyalty to the imperial authority of their respective kingdoms, many of which had the status of federated states, varied according to the political climate. In the end, however, the most damaging blows to the Western Empire, which contributed to its accelerated decline and eventual disappearance, came from those very Germanic 'allies' whom the 'Germanized' Roman army could no longer – or in some cases no longer wanted to – effectively keep in line.

Although the vast majority of the Roman provinces in the West had been gradually transformed or incorporated into Germanic kingdoms since 410, the imperial domain of Italy had, until then, been spared. In fact, at that time, with the exception of the domain of the Roman governor Aegidius, Gaul was divided between the Franks, the Burgundians and the Visigoths; Spain was divided between the Suevi and the Visigoths; North Africa belonged to the Vandals; and Britannia was being conquered by the Angles, the Jutes and the Saxons. In 475, Orestes, who ruled in the name of his young son, had to deliberate on a serious dilemma in this regard. The soldiers of his army, mostly Heruli, wanted in turn to be rewarded for their loyal service with territorial concessions in Italy. Orestes, who was a Roman despite his long association with the Germanic tribes and the Huns, could not consent to such a request. Nor could he compromise by offering in exchange provincial territories that had broken away from the imperial orbit or that were already occupied by other Germanic peoples. The request of the Heruli was therefore simply refused by Orestes, who was strongly supported by the Italian Senate and aristocracy.

An armed revolt ensued among the troops of Orestes, instigated by one of his close lieutenants, Odoacer. Following a short, unequal war between Odoacer's army and Orestes' followers, the latter was defeated and then executed in August 476. The young Romulus was forced to abdicate barely ten months after his ascension. Historians disagree on the real reasons behind Odoacer's decision, but Romulus was not killed. Rather, he was forced to live the rest of his days with his family in the fortress of Neapolis (Naples) on a financial allowance from the State. History is generally unflattering toward Romulus, who most likely lived beyond the year 500. Probably because of his insignificant role in Roman history, in comparison with the Romulus to whom legend attributed the foundation of Rome eleven centuries earlier, Romulus Augustus's name was transformed. Some Byzantine and Renaissance chroniclers added the nickname of 'momyllus' (small disgrace) and even transformed his name *Augustus* into the pejorative diminutive 'Augustulus'. In fact, Romulus who was just a child, was probably unfairly considered.

Romulus's abdication in September 476 marked the official demise of the Western Roman Empire, even though he and his predecessors *Glycerius* and *Julius Nepos* were still alive at that time. The imperial insignia were sent to Constantinople, and the imperial possessions in the West were now part of Germanic kingdoms, except for a few isolated domains that remained Roman for a short time, such as the kingdom of Aegidius in Gaul. It was largely because of this political reality that scholars subsequently recognized the year 476 as the end of antiquity and the beginning of a dark period in the West, corresponding to the first centuries of the Middle Ages.

Divided Empire:
Eastern Emperors (395–491 CE)

Arcadius *Flavius Arcadius*

Cauca (Coca), Spain 377 – Constantinople (Istanbul), Turkey 408
Reign: 395–408

Arcadius was the eldest son of *Theodosius I* and Aelia Flavia Flaccilla. When his brother *Honorius* was born in 383, Arcadius was named *Augustus* at the age of 6. When *Theodosius I* died in 395, Arcadius, then aged 18, succeeded him as head of the Empire in the East, while his younger brother *Honorius*, aged 12, who also had been appointed *Augustus* in 393, assumed the same role in the West. This division of the Empire into two political poles resembled others of the same type in the past, but this time it was significant because it was the prelude to the definitive division of the Roman world. Consequently, the socio-political evolution that characterized each part of the Empire was to follow different paths.

Gold Solidus of Arcadius.

History recognizes Arcadius as the first emperor of what would later be called the Byzantine Empire. While the western part of the Roman Empire did not persist past the end of the fifth century as a political entity, the eastern part was to survive for more than a millennium, undergoing slow but profound transformations along the way. At the end of the fourth century, political and military circumstances forced this divergence.

Despite his maturity, Arcadius did not hold the reins of power. Whether because of his lack of experience related to his youth or the weakness of his character, authority was in the hands of his principal minister and Praetorian prefect, Rufinus, already in the position under *Theodosius I*, and the court chamberlain, Eutropius. Rufinus, although very capable of governing, had a reputation for being unscrupulous, ambitious and a miser. Planning to increase his influence on Arcadius and expand the territory of the East at the expense of the West, he soon entered into conflict with Stilicho, his western counterpart and regent of *Honorius*, who had the same aims, but this time in favour of the West. Moreover, Stilicho claimed that *Theodosius I*, before his death, had given him the charge of watching over his two sons and the Empire. In reality, Stilicho's aim was the annexation of the labour-rich Prefecture of Illyria to the Western Empire.

At the centre of this conflict was a player whose importance would only increase and who would soon make history in a sinister way for the Romans. He was Alaric, the king of the Visigoths. Since 382, the Visigoths had federated status. By a treaty of alliance called *feodus*, the Visigoth nation was officially recognized by the Empire as an equal and independent ally. In exchange for territory within the Empire and recognition of their customs, the Visigoths owed the Empire recruits for military service. But shortly after the death of *Theodosius I*, the federated Visigoths under Alaric's leadership revolted and ravaged the Balkans. Athens was sacked. The situation deteriorated in the East when, at the instigation of Stilicho, Rufinus, who was perhaps preparing to usurp Arcadius's powers, was assassinated. Authority then reverted to Eutropius. Wishing to keep Alaric away from Italy, around 397, Stilicho fought him in Greece, but despite his victory over the Visigoths, Alaric managed to escape. Historians have suggested that Stilicho may have deliberately let him escape in order to keep Alaric in the East and thus harm the interests of Constantinople. As a revolt broke out in Africa against the authority of the West, Eutropius declared the western general-in-chief a public enemy. He was also forced to appoint Alaric, who probably could not be driven out of the East, master of soldiers in the Balkans in order to calm his ambitions. In the West, this double insult caused consternation.

In 399, Stilicho managed to use shenanigans to overthrow Eutropius. Contrary to what one might expect, power still did not fall to Emperor Arcadius. Rather, it was his influential and impulsive wife Aelia Eudoxia who assumed that role after proclaiming herself *Augusta*. In 401, she decided to act against Stilicho by urging Alaric to invade Italy in the name of the East. Alaric was defeated by Stilicho at Pollenza in 402, then again at Verona in 403, but again managed to escape. The following year, Aelia Eudoxia, who had already given birth to a first son with Arcadius in 401, *Theodosius II*, died of a miscarriage. The government then fell into the hands of the Praetorian prefect Anthemius.

Between 404 and 408, there was no decisive military action between East and West, as internal disturbances and invasions required immediate action. In the East, for example, where the situation seemed less critical than in the West, Anthemius had to carry out large-scale campaigns in Southeast Asia Minor (mainland Turkey) to fight bands of Isaurian brigands who were infesting the region.

In 408, at the age of 31, Arcadius died of natural causes, and his son *Theodosius II*, then aged 7, assumed the titular succession. Arcadius's reign was more significant historically for the careers of the leaders of his government than for his emperorship itself. Although we know even less about his private life, some chroniclers describe Arcadius as an individual of rather average intelligence, so as not to use the term mediocre. Otherwise, it is perhaps significant to consider that the succession was still carried out without incident. Unable to govern himself, Arcadius may have had the merit of letting others more gifted do so in his place.

Theodosius II *Flavius Theodosius Junior*

Constantinople (Istanbul), Turkey 401 – Constantinople (Istanbul), Turkey 450
Reign: 408–450

Son of *Arcadius* and Aelia Eudoxia, Theodosius II was proclaimed *Augustus* of the East a few months after his birth to ensure a succession. When *Arcadius* died in 408, Theodosius II, then 7 years old, succeeded him in the custody of a guardian named Antiochus. The transition went smoothly, and the government was in the hands of the first regent and Praetorian prefect Anthemius, who had held the position since 404. Assisted by a friend named Troilus, a pagan sophist known in the rhetorical and philosophical circles of the capital, Anthemius governed energetically and effectively until 414.

The capital's grain supply improved after irregular entries that persisted during the recent troubled years following the Visigoth revolt. Following the disappearance of Stilicho, relations with Ravenna, the capital of the Western Empire, temporarily improved. A new peace treaty with the Persians allowed stability to persist in the more eastern provinces, in Asia Minor as well as in the recently ravaged Danubian provinces. Arrears of uncollected taxes were annulled. The army of the East repelled an invasion of the Huns under Uldin's command. Germanic prisoners who had allied themselves with the Huns were allocated as slaves to landowners in Asia Minor to work the land. The

Gold Solidus of Theodosius II.

sacking of Rome in 410 by the Visigoths and the immediate threat of the Huns prompted Constantinople to enhance its defences. Thus, the fleet stationed on the Danube was strengthened, and Anthemius erected a wall, Theodosius's Wall, around the capital. The wall is still very visible today. The growth of the capital's population had meant that it had long since overflowed the old walls erected by *Constantine I* a century earlier.

In 414, Theodosius II's sister Aelia Pulcheria, aged 16 and two years his senior, was proclaimed *Augusta* and assumed the regency in place of Anthemius, who had disappeared from the chronicles of history. Even Theodosius II's guardian Antiochus was relieved of his duties. Aurelianus became Pulcheria's principal advisor. In 416, Pulcheria arranged the marriage of her brother to the daughter of a sophist named Aelia Eudocia. She and Theodosius II had a daughter, Licinia Eudoxia, who was to later become the wife of *Valentinian III*, future emperor of the West. When in 417 Theodosius II turned 15, which at that time was considered to be the age of maturity, he began to assume his role as emperor despite the influence of his sister during the rest of the reign, which continued in relative stability and prosperity.

In 425, Theodosius II succeeded in overthrowing Emperor *Johannes* and placing his 6-year old cousin *Valentinian III* on the western throne. That same year, he took steps to establish a university in Constantinople. During his reign, Emperor *Constantine I* had founded the School of Stoa, which Emperor *Julian* later enhanced with an important public library. Theodosius II also established seats for Latin and Greek rhetoricians, grammarians, jurists, philosophers and philologists. The predominance of Greek was a prelude to the eventual replacement of Latin as the official language of the Eastern Empire. After eight years of work in association with his western counterpart, Theodosius II published the Theodosian Code of Latin Laws in 438. This collection of imperial laws and decrees dating back more than a century played a major role in the development of Emperor Justinian's code in the following century, a document of law that has been passed down to us.

Despite the efforts of Theodosius II's generals during the last decade of his reign and the payment of large subsidies in order to buy peace, the Danube provinces suffered greatly at the hands of the Huns. In 450, Theodosius II fell while riding a horse and seriously injured his spine. After a forty-two-year reign, Theodosius II succumbed to his injuries. During this long and stable reign, the government leaders laid the foundations of the Byzantine Empire that would last for a millennium. However, his personal impact on the affairs of State was negligible; he was neither a warrior nor a statesman. Chroniclers of the time reported that he was, nonetheless, an intelligent man with a gentle character. Leading a rather secular and morally strict life, he directed his interests toward science, history, astronomy law and theology.

Marcian *Flavius Marcianus*

Place of birth unknown in Thrace 396 – Constantinople (Istanbul), Turkey 457
Reign: 450–457

Son of a soldier of Thracian origin related to *Valentinian I*, Marcian also joined the army. Around 421, he took part in military operations on the border of the Eastern Empire against Persia. Under the command of Ardaburius, he took part in the campaign that led to the overthrow and execution of the Western Emperor *Johannes* in 425 in favour of the elevation of *Valentinian III*. In 431, as a senior officer under the command of Aspar, he was a member of Aetius's failed

Gold Solidus of Marcian.

expedition against the Vandals who were conquering Africa. Taken prisoner, he was released in 434 probably in exchange for a ransom.

When emperor of the East *Theodosius II* died childless in 450, the purple cloak may have been offered to Aspar, now master of soldiers. Some historians suggest that Aspar declined because of his adherence to Arianism. Faced with the possibility of an Arian being elevated to purple cloak (something that had been more acceptable a century before), some influential members of the court would have likely expressed outrage toward Aspar, who was also of Alanic descent. For similar reasons, it would also be reasonable to believe that the spectre of civil disobedience on the part of a significant portion of the population influenced his decision. It was more likely though that Aspar, not being interested in power and its associated perils, deliberately passed the imperial title to one of his closest collaborators. With the consent of the influential Aelia Pulcheria, who then became his wife, Marcian thus rose to the purple cloak, thus continuing the dynasty founded by *Valentinian I* in 364.

Unlike the West, which was shaken by several upheavals during this period, the East was experiencing a cycle of stability and prosperity. Under the reign of Marcian, the Council of Chalcedon held in 451 officially outlawed monophysitism, the doctrine proposing the union of the divine and the human in Christ in one nature.

Relations between East and West, which had remained relatively cordial between *Valentinian III* and *Theodosius II*, began to fester after the death of *Theodosius II* in 450. It all began when *Valentinian III* refused to acknowledge Marcian's elevation. This situation became serious and had tragic consequences for the West after the death of *Valentinian III*. In 455, Marcian refused to send troops to rescue Rome, which was under siege by the Vandals. For the second time in less than fifty years, the Eternal City was taken and plundered. In order to isolate his dominion from the West, Marcian allowed the Ostrogoths and Gepids to settle in Pannonia and part of Illyria.

Marcian's foreign policy was moderate. In order to avoid a war against the Persians, he did not intervene when the Persians invaded Armenia, an ally of the Romans. He may have been right not to engage in a major campaign too far east, as there was a more imminent threat much closer to the capital. Since 450, Marcian had stopped paying the subsidies used to buy peace from the Huns, who had carved out a formidable kingdom just beyond the Danube *limes*. Knowing Attila's reputation, the motives behind Marcian's reluctance to withdraw troops from this vulnerable region may have seemed legitimate. Marcian's fears were justified when Attila decided to invade the Roman Empire in 451. Fortunately for Marcian, it was the West, already suffering the most from the repeated invasions since 406, that became the victim of the wrath of the 'scourge of God'.

Moderation also seemed to have characterized imperial measures internally. Marcian carried out effective financial control without, however, neglecting essential expenditures. Marcian's reign ended in 457 when he died of gout; Pulcheria had died four years earlier. Chroniclers of the time described Marcian's reign as beneficial; some even hinted at a golden age. This statement can be convincing when one compares the stability and prosperity of the East with the disorders that took place in the West at the same time. Marcian was able to please both the aristocracy and the plebeians. The death of the last member of the Valentinian lineage would be regretted for a long time.

Leo I *Flavius Valerius*

Place of birth unknown in Thrace 401 – Constantinople (Istanbul), Turkey 474
Reign: 457–474

When the emperor of the East *Marcian* died in 457, *Anthemius*, who was to become emperor of the West in 467, seemed to be the obvious candidate for succession, but the master of soldiers Aspar did not like him and instead raised one of his own officers to the purple cloak, Leo I, firmly believing that the latter was going to be a puppet ruler. Following a grandiose ceremony in 457, Leo I was the first emperor to be crowned by the Patriarch of Constantinople.

Throughout his reign, Leo I gradually became more and more independent from Aspar and tried to limit Germanic influence in the affairs of State in order for the East to avoid the fate of the West.

Gold Solidus of Leo I.

Since the death of *Valentinian III* in 455, the West was being led by Germanic military generals rather than governed by Roman emperors. One of the best examples of these limiting measures was undoubtedly the formation of the Isaurian Guard in 461. At this period, the recruitment of Roman citizens into the army had become extremely difficult in both spheres of the Empire. In order to counterbalance the growing hold of the Alanic master of soldiers Aspar and his Germanic officers on the affairs of State, Leo I recruited from within the Empire itself. The emphasis was on the recruitment from the mountain people of Isauria, a wild region in southern Asia Minor, in present-day Turkey, whose loyalty was more reliable. In 465, Leo I even gave in marriage his own daughter Aelia Ariadne to one of their leaders, the future Emperor *Zeno*. Without knowing it, Leo I set in motion a process that led to the quasi disappearance of Germanic influence in the East in a span of thirty years. But this deed was of course not to be accomplished without complications.

In collaboration with the new emperor of the West, *Anthemius*, Leo I committed the financial and military resources of the East to a major expedition against the Vandals in 468 and again in 470. The failure of these operations had unfortunate consequences, as they represented the last hopes for the survival of the Western Empire. It had lost most of its territories and was besieged from all sides. In the East, the State coffers were now empty, causing internal tensions. In this unstable environment, the arrival of General *Zeno* at the court of

Constantinople triggered hostilities between his supporters and those of Aspar. While the future emperor *Zeno* was campaigning against the Huns in Thrace and then in Asia Minor, present-day Anatolian Turkey, Aspar forced the appointment of his son as *Caesar* and eventual successor to Leo I. Upon learning the news, *Zeno* returned to the capital and with the assistance of the opposition, outraged to see a Germanic Arian candidate for the purple cloak, overthrew Aspar, who was arrested and killed.

The disappearance of the highest Germanic representative at the court of Constantinople in 471, followed by the promotion of *Zeno* as staff master of soldiers in 473 provoked the revolt of the federated Ostrogoths established in Pannonia by *Marcian*. The Ostrogoths began to ravage the Roman provinces of Mesia, and Leo I had to concede part of this territory to them and pay large subsidies to buy peace. In addition, Leo I gave their leader the title of master of soldiers but limited the scope of the powers associated with that position. In 473 still, Leo I associated to power his 5-year-old grandson Leo II, from the marriage of *Zeno* and Ariadne. Shortly afterwards, Leo I died of dysentery, and before the end of 474, Leo II also died.

Despite the fact that Leo I had been a poorly-educated man, he had been a reasonable and capable emperor. He knew how to limit Germanic influence in the affairs of State, saving the East from the fate of the West, where Roman imperial power was disintegrating. A fervent Christian, he promulgated strict regulations against what remained of pagan practices and Christian heresies. As the Germanic influence in the affairs of State faded away, Arianism lost its predominance in favour of the orthodoxy resulting from the Council of Chalcedon.

Zeno *Flavius Zeno*

Zenopolis (near Elmayurdu), Turkey 425 – Constantinople (Istanbul), Turkey 491
Reign: 474–491
Since the advent of emperor of the East, *Leo I*, in 457, the imperial authorities had been trying to reduce Germanic influence in the army and in the affairs of State. In this way, they were trying to avoid for

Gold Solidus of Zeno.

the East the fate of the West, which was being divided into Germanic kingdoms. The massive enlistment of Isaurian mountaineers replaced the recruitment of Germanic mercenaries. It has been said that the lack of manners and refinement that characterized these Isaurian mountaineers, isolated in the heights of southern Asia Minor, made the Germanic folk, who had long been in contact with the refinement of the Roman world, paled in bellicosity. Nevertheless, the Isaurians were officially citizens of the Empire and their loyalty was more reliable. In 465, *Leo I* even gave in marriage his own daughter Aelia Ariadne to one of their leaders, the future Emperor Zeno.

The disappearance of the master of soldiers Aspar, the highest Germanic representative at the court of Constantinople in 471, the promotion of Zeno as master of soldiers of the staff in 473, and then his elevation to purple cloak shortly after the death of *Leo I* in 474, initiated the revolt of the federated Ostrogoths established in Pannonia and a massive attack by the Vandals in Greece. These disorders barely under control, a conspiracy fomented by Emperor Zeno's political opponents forced him to flee Constantinople to take refuge in Isauria, a region loyal to him in which no one dared to pursue him. These opponents were supported by the pro-Germanic party and a part of the aristocracy and population of the capital who had been troubled by the presence of fierce Isaurians in the capital. The inability of the disunited opponents to agree on the choice of a new emperor permitted the Isaurian party to regain power and bring

Zeno back to the capital. This was all taking place as the Western Roman Empire was disintegrating.

When the Germanic generalissimo Odoacer deposed the last emperor in the West, *Romulus*, and was proclaimed king of Italy in September 476, Zeno, whose authority was still fragile, had no means to intervene. He was therefore forced to recognize Odoacer as king, but summoned him, in vain, to restore the deposed emperor *Julius Nepos* to the throne of the West. Gold coins were minted in the West on which the effigy of *Julius Nepos* as emperor appeared, but Odoacer did nothing more. In reality, even if appearances were temporarily saved, the Western Empire was about to become only a memory, and Zeno could only settle for a fait accompli.

The eradication of the Germanic influence and presence in the East continued under Zeno, with the exception of the Ostrogoths in Pannonia, who were, however, about to leave this region, with the aim of invading Italy under the 'encouragement' of the emperor of the East. But ethnic tensions in Constantinople persisted. The Isaurian presence, better tolerated than that of the Germanic one, was still not unanimously accepted.

On the religious scene, harmony was also conspicuous by its absence. The Council of Chalcedon in 451 condemned monophysitism, which could be summed up as a doctrine affirming the union of the divine and the human in Christ in one nature. This confession nevertheless retained an important influence in the eastern regions of the Empire. It was, moreover, one of the fundamental bases that Islam borrowed almost two centuries later. In the heart of the Empire, Byzantine orthodoxy also gained strength. Religious unrest, in the face of which Zeno remained powerless despite his attempts at compromise, became more complex with the Pope's intervention in Rome, which led to the excommunication of the Patriarch of Constantinople. One must recall that in 444, Emperor *Valentinian III* had put into effect an imperial decree that officially recognized the supremacy of the bishop of Rome over the other bishops of the Empire. This was the birth of the papal concept of the Catholic hierarchy which still exists today. This first schism between these two religious poles of the Christian world was the precursor of a stormy 'ecclesiastical diplomacy' relationship between Rome and Constantinople, which would lead five centuries later to the absolute separation between the Roman Catholic Church and the Greek Orthodox Church.

Until the end of his reign, which ended with his natural death in 491, Zeno ruled an empire shaken by internal conflicts, plots and strong religious dissent. In contrast, the Eastern Roman Empire, which in time would be Hellenized and metamorphosized, was to mark history for another millennium under the appellation of Byzantine Empire.

Glossary

Arianism	doctrine representing Jesus as the son of God without being of the same nature as his father, thus denying the divinity of Christ.
Autocrat, despot	sovereign, absolute monarch.
Bacchanalia	festival dedicated to the god Bacchus; (fam) party that degenerates into an orgy.
Chamberlain	senior civil servant in charge of the personal and private services of the emperor.
Congiarium	distribution of food or monetary donations to the plebeians or soldiers.
Consul	elected magistrate who shares with another the supreme authority. A proconsul is an outgoing consul whose powers are extended to continue an ongoing military campaign or to govern a province. During the Roman Empire, every governor of a senatorial province had the title of proconsul.
Dominate	phase of the Roman Empire corresponding to the period from the exclusive reign of Diocletian starting in 285 CE to the fall of the Western Roman Empire in 476 CE. It is considered as more authoritarian, more bureaucratic and less collaborative than the previous Principate period.
Equestrian order	class of Roman citizens below the senatorial order.
Limes	fortified borders of the Roman Empire with no natural defences.
Paganism	name given by the first Christians to those who recognize several deities.
Patrician	member of the aristocratic class.
Pax romana	century between the reign of Trajan (98–177) and that of Severus Alexander (222–235), which corresponds to the apogee of Roman civilization.
Plebeian	member of the popular class.
Prefect	senior administrative or military official.
Prefect of the Praetorium	senior military official and close collaborator of the emperor.

Principate	phase of the Roman Empire corresponding to the period from the reign of Augustus in 27 BCE to the advent of the exclusive reign of Diocletian starting in 285 CE. This period is characterized by the reign of a single emperor (or princeps) and is aimed at preserving the illusion of continuity of the Republic.
Purple cloak	garment, sheet dyed purple and symbol of authority; dignity of consuls and other sovereign magistrates under the Republic; designation of the emperor under the imperial regime.
Quaestor	senior government finance official.
Rhetorician	professor, master of public speaking.
Sedition	premeditated revolt against authority.
Servile	relating to slavery, to the status of servant.
Syncretism	philosophical or religious concept that advocates the fusion of different doctrines.
Theocratic	political authority where law and religion merge.
Universalism	concept of collective homogeneity.
Usurpation	illegitimate appropriation of a property, of an authority.

Table of Illustrations

Gold Aureus of Valerius Severus, p. 88 (With permission of wildwinds. com, ex Numismatica Ars Classica)

Gold Medallion of 4 Aurei of Maxentius, p. 88 (With permission of wildwinds.com, ex Numismatica Ars Classica)

Bronze Follis of Licinius, p. 89 (Courtesy of Chip Gruszczinski)

Gold Aureus of Maximinus II Daia, p. 89 (With permission of wildwinds. com)

Gold Solidus of Constantine I, p. 90 (With permission of wildwinds.com, ex Numismatica Ars Classica)

Statue of the Tetrarchy in Venice in 1995, p. 92 (Photograph from the author)

Statue of the Tetrarchy in Venice in 2010, p. 93 (Photograph from the author)

Arch of Constantine I in Rome, p. 100 (Photograph from the author)

Bronze coin of Constantine II, p. 102 (Courtesy of Chip Gruszczinski)

Bronze coin of Constans, p. 104 (Courtesy of Chip Gruszczinski)

Coin of Constantius II, p. 106 (Private collection)

Silver 9 Siliquae coin of Magnentius, p. 109 (With permission of wildwinds. com, ex Numismatica Ars Classica)

Silver Siliqua of Julian, p. 110 (Courtesy of Chip Gruszczinski)

Bronze coin of Jovian, p. 113 (Courtesy of Chip Gruszczinski)

Gold Solidus of Valentinian I, p. 115 (Courtesy of Chip Gruszczinski)

Gold Solidus of Valens, p. 118 (With permission of wildwinds.com, ex CNG Coins and Triton Auctions)

Gold 1.5 Scripula of Gratian, p. 120 (With permission of wildwinds.com)

Bronze coin of Valentinian II, p. 122 (Courtesy of Chip Gruszczinski)

Gold Solidus of Magnus Maximus, p. 124 (With permission of wildwinds. com, ex Numismatica Ars Classica)

Bronze coin of Theodosius I, p. 126 (Private collection)

Gold Solidus of Honorius, p. 129 (With permission of wildwinds.com, ex CNG Coins and Triton Auctions)

Gold Solidus of Constantius III, p. 133 (With permission of wildwinds. com, ex CNG Coins and Triton Auctions)

Gold Solidus of Johannes, p. 134 (With permission of wildwinds.com, ex CNG Coins and Triton Auctions)

Gold Tremissis of Valentinian III, p. 136 (Courtesy of Chip Gruszczinski)

Gold Solidus of Petronus Maximus, p. 139 (With permission of wildwinds. com, ex CNG Coins and Triton Auctions)

Gold Tremissis of Avitus, p. 141 (With permission of wildwinds.com, ex CNG Coins and Triton Auctions)

Gold Solidus of Majorian, p. 143 (With permission of wildwinds.com, ex Roma Numismatics auction XIX)

Gold Solidus of Libius Severus, p. 145 (With permission of wildwinds.com)

Alphabetical Table

Note: Terms in capital letters refer to narratives that do not correspond to emperors.

Bibliography

Austin, N.J.E., and Rankov, N., *Exploratio: Military and Political Intelligence in the Roman World from the Second Punic War to the Battle of Adrianople* (London: Routledge, 1995).

Bartolini, M., *L'espion devenu empereur : Procope d'après Ammien Marcellin*, Histoire Antique, Éditions Faton, France, No 31, (Mai-Juin 2007), pp. 62–67.

Bartolini, M., *Ammien Marcellin et le renseignement extérieur romain*, Scripta Mediterranea, Volume XXIV, (2004), pp. 3–19.

Bartolini, M., *Apport stratégique au déclin de l'armée romaine : la grande stratégie de défense en profondeur*, Histoire Antique, Éditions Harnois, Part I, No.12, (Décembre 2003–Janvier 2004), pp.58–65; Part II, No.13, (Février-Mars 2004), pp. 64–67.

Bartolini, M., *Les causes du changement de la grande stratégie romaine de défense périphérique à la défense en profondeur au IIIe siècle*, Ancient History Bulletin, volume 17.3–4, (2003), pp.195–212.

Besnier, M., *L'empire romain de l'avènement des Sévère au Concile de Nicée* (Paris: Presses Universitaires de France, 1937).

Brauer, G., *The Age of the Soldier-Emperors* (Park Ridge, New Jersey: Noyes Press, 1975).

Bunson, M., *A Dictionary of the Roman Empire* (New York: Oxford University Press, 1991).

Chastagnol, A., *Histoire Auguste, Les empereurs romains des IIe et IIIe siècles* (Paris, coll., Robert Laffont, 1994).

Coarelli, F., *Guide archéologique de Rome* (Paris: Hachette, 1994).

Cowan, R., *Roman Battle Tactics 109 BC – AD 313* (Oxford: Osprey, 2013).

Cowan, R., *Roman Legionary AD 284–337* (Oxford: Osprey, 2015).

Dando-Collins, S., *Legions of Rome* (New York: St Martin's Press, 2012).

Demat, M., et Laloup, J., *À la découverte du monde gréco-romain,* Tomes 1 et 2, Liège (H. Dessain, 1963).

Dodgeon, M., *The Roman Eastern Frontier and the Persian Wars AD 226–363* (London: Routledge, 1991).

Ferrill, A., *Roman Imperial Grand Strategy* (Lanham: University Press of America, 1991).

Ferrill, A., *The Fall of the Roman Empire: The Military Explanation* (London: Thames & Hudson Ltd, 1988).

Garnsey, P., and Saller, R., *The Roman Empire: Economy, Society, Culture* (London, 1987).

Garzetti, A., *From Tiberius to the Antonines* (London: Methuen, 1974).

Gibbon, E., *The Decline and Fall of the Roman Empire*, Vol. 1 to 6 (London, J.M. Dent & Sons Ltd, 1929).

Goldsworthy, A., *In the Name of Rome: The Men who Won the Roman Empire* (London: Phoenix, 2003).

Hacquard, G., *Guide Romain Antique* (Paris: Hachette, 1952).

Hildinger, E., *Swords against the Senate* (Cambridge: Perseus Books Group, 2003).

Isaac, B., *The Limits of Empire: The Roman Army in the East* (Oxford: 1990).

Jones, A.H.M., *The Later Roman Empire, 284–602: A Social, Economic and Administrative Survey* (Oxford: Blackwell, 1964).

Lee, A., *Information and Frontiers: Roman Foreign Relations in Late Antiquity* (Cambridge: Cambridge University Press, 1993).

Le Glay, M., *Rome, grandeur et chute de l'Empire* (Paris: Perrin, 1992).

Linder, R.P., 'Nomadism, Horses and Huns', *Past & Present*, 92, (1981).

Luttwak, E., *The Grand Strategy of the Roman Empire* (Baltimore: The John Hopkins University Press, 1979).

O'Flynn, J.M., *Generalissimos of the Western Roman Empire* (Edmonton: The University of Alberta Press, 1983).

Scarre, C., *Chronique des empereurs romains* (Paris: Casterman, 1995).

Simkins, M., and Youens, M., *The Roman Army from Caesar to Trajan* (Berkshire: Osprey Publishing Ltd, 1974).

Sinnigen, W., 'Two Branches of the Late Roman Secret Service', *American Journal of Philology*, 80, (1961).

Southern, P., and Dixon, K., *The Late Roman Army* (New Haven: Yale University Press, 1996).

Todd, M., *Les Germains: Aux frontières de l'Empire romain 100 av. J.-C. – 300 ap. J.C.* (Paris: Armand Colin, 1990).

Wells, C., *The Roman Empire* (Glasgow: William Collins Sons & Co. Ltd., 1984).

Wheeler, E.L., 'Methodological Limits and Mirage of Roman Strategy: Part I', *The Journal of Military History*, 57, (January 1993).

Windrow, M., and McBride, A., *Imperial Rome at War* (Hong Kong: Concord Publications Co., 1996.)

Zosso, F., et Zingg, C., *Les empereurs romains 27 av. J.-C. – 476 ap. J.-C.* (Paris: Errance, 1994).